PENGUIN MODERN CLASSICS

Lady Sings the Blues

Billie Holiday was born in 1915. She began singing in jazz clubs in Harlem while still a teenager, never undergoing technical training or even learning to read music. Mainstream success followed with hits like *Summertime*, *Autumn in New York* and *Strange Fruit*. To this day she is still considered by many to be the greatest jazz singer of all time. She died in 1959, aged 44.

BILLIE HOLIDAY

Lady Sings the Blues

Written with William Dufty

PENGUIN BOOKS

PENGUIN CLASSICS

UK | USA | Canada | Ireland | Australia
India | New Zealand | South Africa

Penguin Books is part of the Penguin Random House group of companies
whose addresses can be found at global.penguinrandomhouse.com.

First published by Doubleday, a division of Random House, Inc. 1956
This edition published in Penguin Classics 2018
009

Set in 10.5/13 pt Dante MT Std
Typeset by Jouve (UK), Milton Keynes
Printed and bound in Italy by Grafica Veneta S.p.A.

A CIP catalogue record for this book is available from the British Library

ISBN: 978-0-241-35129-1

www.greenpenguin.co.uk

MIX
Paper from
responsible sources
FSC® C018179

Penguin Random House is committed to a
sustainable future for our business, our readers
and our planet. This book is made from Forest
Stewardship Council® certified paper.

Lady Sings the Blues

I

Some Other Spring

Mom and Pop were just a couple of kids when they got married. He was eighteen, she was sixteen, and I was three.

Mom was working as a maid with a white family. When they found out she was going to have a baby they just threw her out. Pop's family just about had a fit, too, when they heard about it. They were real society folks and they never heard of things like that going on in their part of East Baltimore.

But both kids were poor. And when you're poor, you grow up fast.

It's a wonder my mother didn't end up in the workhouse and me as a foundling. But Sadie Fagan loved me from the time I was just a swift kick in the ribs while she scrubbed floors. She went to the hospital and made a deal with the head woman there. She told them she'd scrub floors and wait on the other bitches laying up there to have their kids so she could pay her way and mine. And she did. Mom was thirteen that Wednesday, April 7, 1915, in Baltimore when I was born.

By the time she worked her way out of hock in the hospital and took me home to her folks, I was so big and smart I could sit up in a carriage. Pop was doing what all the boys did then – peddling papers, running errands, going to school. One day he came along by my carriage, picked me up and started playing with me. His mother saw him and came hollering. She dragged at him and said, 'Clarence, stop playing with that baby. Everybody is going to think it's yours.'

'But, Mother, it *is* mine,' he'd tell her. When he talked back to his mother like this she would really have a fit. He was still only fifteen and in short pants. He wanted to be a musician and used to take lessons on the trumpet. It was almost three years before he got long pants for the wedding.

After they were married awhile we moved into a little old house on Durham Street in Baltimore. Mom had worked as a maid up North in New York and Philly. She'd seen all the rich people with their gas and electric lights and she decided she had to have them too. So she saved her wages for the day. And when we moved in we were the first family in the neighborhood to have gas and electricity.

It made the neighbors mad, Mom putting in the gas. They said putting pipes in the ground would bring the rats out. It was true. Baltimore is famous for rats.

Pop always wanted to blow the trumpet but he never got the chance. Before we got one to blow, the Army grabbed him and shipped him overseas. It was just his luck to be one of the ones to get it from poison gas over there. It ruined his lungs. I suppose if he'd played piano he'd probably have got shot in the hand.

Getting gassed was the end of his hopes for the trumpet but the beginning of a successful career on the guitar. He started to learn it when he was in Paris. And it was a good thing he did. Because it kept him from going to pieces when he got back to Baltimore. He just *had* to be a musician. He worked like hell when he got back and eventually got a job with McKinney's Cotton Pickers. But when he went on the road with that band it was the beginning of the end of our life as a family. Baltimore got to be just another one-night stand.

While Pop was overseas in the war, Mom had worked in a factory making Army overalls and uniforms. When Pop hit the road, the war jobs were finished and Mom figured she could do better going off up North as a maid. She had to leave me with my grandparents, who lived in a poor little old house with my cousin Ida, her two small children, Henry and Elsie, and my great-grandmother.

All of us were crowded in that little house like fishes. I had to sleep in the same bed with Henry and Elsie, and Henry used to wet it every night. It made me mad and sometimes I'd get up and sit in a chair until morning. Then my cousin Ida would come in in the morning, see the bed, accuse me of wetting it, and start beating me. When she was upset she'd beat me something awful. Not with a strap, not with a spank on the ass, but with her fists or a whip.

She just didn't understand me. Other kids, when they did something wrong, would lie their way out of it. But if I did anything wrong I'd come right out and admit it. And she'd have a fit, call me a sinner and tell me I'd never amount to anything. She never got through telling my mother I was going to bring home a baby and disgrace the damn family like she did. One time she heard me say 'Damn it' and she thought this was so sinful she tossed a pot of hot starch at me. She missed, though, because I ducked.

She was always finding fault with whatever I did, but she never did pick up on Henry. He was her son and he could do no wrong. When I got tired of getting beaten because he wet the bed I got Elsie one night and convinced her we should both sleep on the floor. She was scared. It was cold and she thought we might freeze.

'All right,' I told her, 'so we might freeze. But if we ain't frozen to death in the morning, the bed'll be wet and we won't be in it.'

It was and we weren't, so this time Cousin Ida beat me for being smart with her. 'Henry's weak,' she said.

You couldn't tell her nothing about Henry, why that boy used to give us girls a terrible time. He even tried to do what we called 'that thing' to us while we were sleeping. Sometimes we would be so tired from fighting this little angel off all night, we wouldn't wake up in time for school. I used to try to plead with him because I knew it wouldn't do any good to talk to Cousin Ida.

'Henry,' I'd say to him, 'it ain't so bad with me. I'm only your cousin. But Elsie's your sister, and besides, she's sick.'

Henry grew up to be a prize fighter and then a minister. But when he was little I had hell with that boy.

One day we were playing baseball and afterwards I was sitting on the curb. I was scared of the tiniest bugs, anything that crawled, and Henry knew it. This day he came up to me holding one of Baltimore's biggest goddamn rats by the tail, swinging it in my face.

'Don't do that, Henry,' I begged him.

'What's the matter, you scared?' he said, grinning and swinging it closer and closer to me.

'All girls is scared of rats and bugs,' I said.

He kept right on swinging. Finally he hit me in the face with the rat. I took a baseball bat and put him in the Johns Hopkins Hospital.

I don't think my grandma ever understood me either, but she never beat me like Cousin Ida did, and that was something. My grandpop loved me, though. He was half Irish and named after his father, Charles Fagan, who was straight from Ireland.

The one I really liked best, though, was my great-grandmother, my grandfather's mother.

She really loved me and I was crazy about her. She had been a slave on a big plantation in Virginia and she used to tell me about it. She had her own little house in the back of the plantation. Mr Charles Fagan, the handsome Irish plantation owner, had his white wife and children in the big house. And he had my great-grandmother out in back. She had sixteen children by him, and all of them were dead by then except Grandpop.

We used to talk about life. And she used to tell me how it felt to be a slave, to be owned body and soul by a white man who was the father of her children. She couldn't read or write, but she knew the Bible by heart from beginning to end and she was always ready to tell me a story from the Scriptures.

She was ninety-six or ninety-seven then and had dropsy. I used to take care of her every day after school. No one else paid any attention. I'd give her a bath sometimes. And I'd always bind her legs with fresh cloths and wash the smelly old ones.

She'd been sleeping in chairs for ten years. The doctor had told her she'd die if ever she laid down. But I didn't know. And once after I'd changed the cloths on her legs and she had told me a story, she begged me to let her lie down. She said she was tired. I didn't want to let her. But she kept begging and begging. It was pitiful.

Finally I spread a blanket on the floor and helped her stretch out. Then she asked me to lie down with her because she wanted to tell me another story. I was tired too. I'd been up early that morning to scrub steps. So I laid down with her. I don't remember the story she told me because I fell asleep right away.

I woke up four or five hours later. Grandma's arm was still tight around my neck and I couldn't move it. I tried and tried and then I got scared. She was dead, and I began to scream. The neighbors came running. They had to break Grandma's arm to get me loose. Then they took me to a hospital. I was there for a month. Suffering from what they said was shock.

When I got home Cousin Ida started right in where she had left off, beating me. This time it was for letting Grandma out of her chair. The doctor tried to stop her. He said if she kept it up I'd grow up to be nervous. But she never stopped.

I was a woman when I was sixteen. I was big for my age, with big breasts, big bones, a big fat healthy broad, that's all. So I started working out then, before school and after, minding babies, running errands, and scrubbing those damn white steps all over Baltimore.

When families in the neighborhood used to pay me a nickel for scrubbing them down, I decided I had to have more money, so I figured out a way. I bought me a brush of my own, a bucket, some rags, some Octagon soap, and a big white bar of that stuff I can't ever forget – Bon Ami.

The first time I stood on a white doorstep and asked this woman for fifteen cents for the job, she like to had a fit. But I explained to her the higher price came from me bringing my own supplies. She thought I had a damn nerve, I guess, but while she was thinking it over I said I'd scrub the kitchen or bathroom floor for the same price. That did it. I had the job.

All these bitches were lazy. I knew it and that's where I had them. They didn't care how filthy their damn houses were inside, as long as those white steps were clean. Sometimes I'd bring home as much as ninety cents a day. I even made as high as $2.10 – that's fourteen kitchen or bathroom floors and as many sets of steps.

When I went into the scrubbing business it was the end of roller skating, bike riding, and boxing, too. I used to like boxing. In school they used to teach us girls to box. But I didn't keep it up. Once a girl hit me on the nose and it just about finished me. I took my gloves off and beat the pants off her. The gym teacher got so sore, I never went near the school gym again.

But whether I was riding a bike or scrubbing somebody's dirty bathroom floor, I used to love to sing all the time. I liked music. If there was a place where I could go and hear it, I went.

Alice Dean used to keep a whorehouse on the corner nearest our place, and I used to run errands for her and the girls. I was very commercial in those days. I'd never go to the store for anybody for less than a nickel or a dime. But I'd run all over for Alice and the girls, and I'd wash basins, put out the Lifebuoy soap and towels. When it came time to pay me, I used to tell her she could keep the money if she'd let me come up in her front parlor and listen to Louis Armstrong and Bessie Smith on her victrola.

A victrola was a big deal in those days, and there weren't any parlors around that had one except Alice's. I spent many a wonderful hour there listening to Pops and Bessie. I remember Pops' recording of 'West End Blues' and how it used to gas me. It was the first time I ever heard anybody sing without using any words. I didn't know he was singing whatever came into his head when he forgot the lyrics. Ba-ba-ba-ba-ba-ba-ba and the rest of it had plenty of meaning for me – just as much meaning as some of the other words that I didn't always understand. But the meaning used to change, depending on how I felt. Sometimes the record would make me so sad I'd cry up a storm. Other times the same damn record would make me so happy I'd forget about how much hard-earned money the session in the parlor was costing me.

But Mom didn't favor her daughter hanging around the house on the corner. And especially she couldn't understand why I wasn't bringing home any loot. 'I know Eleanora,' she used to complain, Eleanora being the name I'd been baptized under, 'and she don't work for nobody for nothing.' When Mom found out I was using my hard-earned money paying rent on Alice's parlor to listen to jazz on the victrola, she nearly had a fit too.

I guess I'm not the only one who heard their first good jazz in a whorehouse. But I never tried to make anything of it. If I'd heard Louis and Bessie at a Girl Scout jamboree, I'd have loved it just the same. But a lot of white people first heard jazz in places like Alice Dean's, and they helped label jazz 'whorehouse music.'

They forget what it was like in those days. A whorehouse was about the only place where black and white folks could meet in any natural way. They damn well couldn't rub elbows in the churches. And in Baltimore, places like Alice Dean's were the only joints fancy enough to have a victrola and for real enough to pick up on the best records.

I know this for damn sure. If I'd heard Pops and Bessie wailing through the window of some minister's front parlor, I'd have been running free errands for him. There weren't any priests in Baltimore then like Father Norman O'Connor of Boston, who loves jazz and now has a big radio congregation listening to his disc-jockey shows.

About the only other place you could hear music those days was at dances. So I used to go to as many dances as I could get near. Not to dance, just to listen to the band. You couldn't expect Cousin Ida to believe that, though. She accused me of staying off the dance floor so I could hang around the edges and pick up boys. So she'd beat me for that too.

She was always worried about me and boys. We lived next door to a junk shop. The junk wagon was always parked in front after making the rounds that day. The neighborhood boys used to hang around in the junk wagon shooting marbles and dice. And I used to hang around with them. I used to shoot with them and fight with them, but that's all. One day a nosy old lady hung herself out a second-story window and started shaking her finger at me. Then she came down and hollered at me, saying I was a disgrace to the neighborhood for what I was doing with the boys.

I had no eyes for sex and I was doing nothing with the boys that another boy couldn't do. I was one of the boys. So when this nosy old bitch shook her finger at me I hollered right back. 'You think I'm doing that thing with them, don't you?' I asked her.

When she heard the naughty word she forgot what she was raising hell about and started hollering about my language. She thought it was terrible for me to say what she had been thinking. I didn't care about what she thought, or anybody. But I didn't want her worrying my mother. Because I knew my mother worried.

'You ain't got no father,' she used to tell me. 'I work so hard. Please don't make the same mistake I made.'

She was always afraid I'd end up bad and there would be nothing she could say. She never hit me when she thought I was doing something bad. She would just cry, and I couldn't stand to see her cry. I didn't want to hurt her, and I didn't – until three years before she died, when I went on junk.

But back then I was worried what this old bitch might tell my mother. So when she told me she thought I was doing the thing with those boys and I wasn't, I picked up a broom and beat her until she agreed to tell my mother she had never seen me doing nothing with the boys.

The boys were doing it, though. And they were looking for some girl who would. And I could tell them who. The one who was always a sure thing was the saintliest girl on the block. She always kept saying she was going to be a great dancer; meantime she was doing it, not only with the boys but with all those women's husbands.

But she was always so damn proper and saintly, this Evelyn, she wouldn't say 'Bon Ami' if she had a mouthful. But because my mother had made a mistake, everybody, including Cousin Ida, was always raising hell with me.

I went back to Baltimore a few years ago when I was playing the Royale Theatre. I drove up in my white Cadillac in front of the house where Evelyn used to live. I parked it where the junk wagon used to sit. This saintly bitch who was going to be a big dancer was still living there. She had six kids and none of them by the same father and she was still funky and greasy. The kids lined up in the street and I bought them ice cream and gave them fifty cents apiece. They thought it was a big deal and I was a big star.

Evelyn always kept a young cat in the house and she had one that day, young and brown and good-looking. He leaned out the window, pointed to one of the six kids, and said, 'This one is mine.' I never forgot that day. These were the people who used to worry me and Mom to death about going bad.

There were other things I missed when I went into the scrubbing business full time. I used to love to go to the five-and-dime store in Baltimore and buy hot dogs. They never used to wait on Negroes there. But they'd sell me a hot dog because I was a kid and

I guess they could use the business if nobody was looking. But if they caught me eating that hot dog before I got outside on the street, they'd give me hell for cluttering up the place.

I used to love white silk socks, too, and of course black patent-leather shoes. I could never afford them. But I used to sneak in the five-and-dime and grab the white socks off the counter and run like hell. Why not? They wouldn't let me buy them even if I did have the money.

I learned to crawl in the back way at the movies to save the dime it cost going in the front way. I don't think I missed a single picture Billie Dove ever made. I was crazy for her. I tried to do my hair like her and eventually I borrowed her name.

My name, Eleanora, was too damn long for anyone to say. Besides, I never liked it. Especially not after my grandma shortened it and used to scream 'Nora!' at me from the back porch. My father had started calling me Bill because I was such a young tomboy. I didn't mind that, but I wanted to be pretty, too, and have a pretty name. So I decided Billie was it and I made it stick.

All the time Mom worked in Philly and New York she used to send me clothes given her by the white people she worked for. They were hand-me-downs, sure, but they were beautiful and I was always the sharpest kid in the block when I was dressed up.

My mother knew I didn't like it much living with my grandparents and Cousin Ida. She didn't like it any better. But the only damn thing she could do about it was work as hard as she could up North and save every nickel. So this is what she did.

After Pop went on the road with McKinney's Cotton Pickers, he just disappeared. Later he got a job with Fletcher Henderson's band. But he was always on tour, and then one day we heard that he had gotten a divorce and married a West Indian woman named Fanny.

When my mother came back to Baltimore one day she had nine hundred dollars she had saved. She bought a real fancy house on Pennsylvania Avenue in North Baltimore, the high-class part. She was going to take in roomers. We were going to live like ladies and everything was going to be fine.

★

All the big-time whores wore big red velvet hats then with bird-of-paradise feathers on them. These lids were the thing. You couldn't touch one for less than twenty-five dollars – a lot of money in the twenties. I always wanted Mom to have one, and when she finally made it I loved it so I'd throw a fit unless she wore it from the time she got up in the morning until she went to bed at night. If she left the house without it, I'd carry on. She looked so pretty in it, and I thought she should look pretty all the time. She was no more than five feet tall and she weighed less than eighty pounds. In her red velvet bird-of-paradise hat she looked like a living doll.

When she went out in this fancy outfit she'd always talk about getting a rich husband so both of us working girls could retire. But her heart was never in it.

A while after Pop had married again Mom met Phil Gough. He was a Baltimore longshoreman but he came from a very high-class family. His sisters were all office workers, and besides, they were very light-skinned and thought it was terrible he was taking up with Mom and me, because we were a shade or two darker.

But he didn't pay any attention to that. He married Mom anyway and he was a good stepdaddy to me as long as he lived, which was only a little while.

I was happy for a little bit. It couldn't last.

One day when I came home from school Mom was at the hairdresser's and there was nobody in the house but Mr Dick, one of our neighbors. He told me Mother had asked him to wait for me and then take me a few blocks away to somebody's house, where she would meet us.

Without me thinking anything about it, he took me by the hand and I went along. When we got to the house, a woman let us in. I asked for my mother and they said she would be along soon. I think they told me she had called them on the telephone and said she would be late. It got later and later and I began to get sleepy. Mr Dick saw me dozing and took me into a back bedroom to lie down. I was almost asleep when Mr Dick crawled up on me and started trying to do what my cousin Henry used to try. I started to kick and scream like crazy. When I did, the woman of the house came in and tried to hold my head and arms down on the bed so he could get at me. I gave both of them a hard time, kicking and scratching and screaming. Suddenly, when I was catching my breath, I heard some more hollering and shouting. The next thing I knew, my mother and a policeman broke the door down. I'll never forget that night. Even if you're a whore, you don't want to be raped. A bitch can turn twenty-five hundred tricks a day and she still don't want nobody to rape her. It's the worst thing that can happen to a woman. And here it was happening to me when I was ten.

I couldn't figure out how my mother had managed to find where they had taken me. But when she had come home, one of Mr Dick's girl friends, a jealous hustler, was waiting on the porch. She warned Mom to keep me away from her man.

Mom tried to brush her off, telling her I was just a kid and to quit being jealous and silly.

'Just a kid?' said this hustler, laughing. 'She ran off with my man. She's with him right now, and if you don't believe me I'll tell you where you'll find them.'

Mom didn't waste no time. She called the police and took this jealous bitch by the arm and dragged her to the house where they had me. And a house it was, too.

But that wasn't the worst of it. The cops dragged Dick off to the police precinct. I was crying and bleeding in my mother's arms, but they made us come along too.

When we got there instead of treating me and Mom like somebody who called the cops for help, they treated me like I'd killed somebody. They wouldn't let my mother take me home. Mr Dick was in his forties, and I was only ten. Maybe the police sergeant took one look at my breasts and limbs and figured my age from that. I don't know. Anyway, I guess they had me figured for having enticed this old goat into the whorehouse or something. All I know for sure is they threw me into a cell. My mother cried and screamed and pleaded, but they just put her out of the jailhouse and turned me over to a fat white matron. When she saw I was still bleeding, she felt sorry for me and gave me a couple of glasses of milk. But nobody else did anything for me except give me filthy dirty looks and snicker to themselves.

After a couple of days in a cell they dragged me into court. Mr Dick got sentenced to five years. They sentenced me to a Catholic institution.

I'll never forget that place. It is run by the Catholic sisters, the kind who never go outside the four walls. When you go in they give you a blue and white uniform and a saint's name. I drew the name of St Theresa. There were about a hundred girls there, mostly for stealing and hooking from school. But they knew I was there on account of a man, so they all looked up to me as some kind of a big shot.

When you did something against the rules at that place, at least they didn't beat you, like Cousin Ida had. When you were being punished you got a raggedy red dress to wear. When you wore this dress, none of the other girls were supposed to go near you or speak to you.

I'll never forget the first girl I saw wear the dress. She was a real wild one and she was alone in the back yard, standing on a swing. She kept swinging higher and higher, shouting and hollering, swinging higher and higher. She worked so hard she was puffing and huffing. And the kids stood around watching her, all eyes.

The Mother Superior tried to keep the kids moving and break up the crowd of gawking girls. The girl in the raggedy red dress just kept on swinging and screaming. I guess she figured as long as she stayed up there on the swing no one could touch her. The Mother Superior looked at her, then she turned to a group of us and said: 'Just remember, God will punish her. God will punish her.'

In a few seconds there was a terrible jerk. As she swung to the highest point she could make on the swing, the chair broke and the girl flew through the air, over the fence, screaming as she sailed through the air. Then there was a terrible thud and then nothing. When they found her, her neck was broken.

The first time I wore the red dress was at Easter. My mother came to visit me and she brought a huge basket, two fried chickens, a dozen hard-boiled eggs, and all kinds of things. Because I had the red dress on, the sisters gave my basket to the other girls and made me sit there and watch them while they ate it.

But this wasn't punishment enough. They wouldn't let me sleep in the dormitory with the other girls. Another girl had died and they had her laid out in the front room. And for punishment they locked me in the room with her for the night. Maybe it was the girl who broke her neck on the swing. I don't really remember. All I knew was I couldn't stand dead people ever since my great-grandmother had died holding me in her arms. I couldn't sleep. I couldn't stand it. I screamed and banged on the door so, I kept the whole joint from sleeping. I hammered on the door until my hands were bloody.

The next time my mother came to visit me I told her if she ever wanted to see me again she better get me out of there. I guess she knew I meant it. And I did. Anyway, she and Grandpop got a lawyer. Some rich white people my mother was working for helped her out too. According to the judge, I was supposed to stay there until I was dead or twenty-one. But they finally got me out.

I went back there once years later, when I needed some proof I had been born before I could get a passport to go abroad. I came back to see the Mother Superior.

I had told the government people about being born in that hospital in Baltimore where my mother scrubbed floors and carried water when she was only thirteen, but they wouldn't believe me. The same Mother Superior was there who had been there thirty years before. And I saw the place where I had slept, the place I was baptized, the place I was confirmed, and the place where I had beaten my hands to a bloody damn pulp when they put me in a raggedy red dress and locked me up with the body of a dead girl.

2

Ghost of Yesterdays

Everybody was talking about Lindbergh's hop to Paris that summer of 1927 when I made it solo from Baltimore to New York.

From the day she got me sprung from the Catholic institution, Mom and I were drug with Baltimore. We had had it with roomers after the deal with Mr Dick. There was nothing to do except for Mom to go back slaving away as somebody's maid. In Baltimore she couldn't make half the loot she could up North. So I dragged my scrub brush and bucket from house to house trying to make up the difference that could keep us together.

One night I came home long after dark. I had worked all day and had ninety cents to show for it. Mom took one look at me and busted out crying, I looked that beat. I tried to comfort her and tell her I'd be all right, but she kept saying, 'There's got to be something better than this.' And if there was, she and I knew it had to be up North. It wasn't going to be in Baltimore.

So up she went. And back I went into the little house with Cousin Ida and her husband, Grandma and Grandpop, little Cousin Henry and Elsie – to wait for the day Mom could send for me to come to New York.

Life with Cousin Ida was just more of the same. I couldn't wait for it to be over, and then I hated the way it ended. She was one of the worst black bitches God ever put on earth, but I hated the way she died. Goiters ran in my mother's family; Mom had one, but Cousin Ida's was the worse, a great big horrible one that hung from her chin to her breast. One day she had a choking spell and there was nobody around to help her but her husband, and he was passed out drunk. She died like a dog, on her knees, choking for air. The doctor said if her man had even come to enough to raise the window and let in some air he could have saved her. But he was too juiced even for that. Mean as she was, I hated to see her die like that.

In those days they kept dead bodies around for two weeks for the waking and crying. Cousin Ida and her husband were Baptists and they gave Mom and me a hard time because we were Catholic. We were always accused of thinking we were better than the Baptists. They used to make fun of Mom with her candles and creeping up to the altar. So when I refused to look at Cousin Ida's body they thought it had something to do with that. They wouldn't let me alone. Finally, when I wouldn't go near the coffin, someone dragged me over by it, held me up, and made me look at her. I was sick from that.

With Cousin Ida dead and nobody to look after Henry and Elsie, let alone me, Mom sent for me to come to New York. I finished up the fifth grade, and as soon as school was out Grandpop put one of those big tags around my neck, saying who I was and where I was going. Grandma made me this big basket of fried chicken, hard-boiled eggs – enough food to last Lindbergh across the Atlantic. And Grandpop put me on the train. I had a ticket to Long Branch, where Mom was going to meet me. But as soon as I got on the train by myself I decided, damn Long Branch, I was going to get to see Harlem someway. So I took off the big tag, decided I'd get off the train in New York, take the subway to Harlem, have myself a time, and then contact my mother.

I was only thirteen, but I was a hip kitty. I was traveling light – except for that basket of chicken – but I was traveling. When I got off at Pennsylvania Station in New York, I had never seen a place so big. I was wandering around, taking my own sweet time, looking at all the big buildings, taking it all in. I must have been a sight, traipsing around, gawking, with this basket of chicken and my little suitcase. Anyway, this social worker spotted me and she knew damn well I was lost.

It was dark by then. This social worker was white, but she was nice as she could be. She asked me where I had come from, what my name was, where I was going, who my mother was, and all that stuff. But I wouldn't tell her anything, not even my name. Nobody was going to stop me from getting to Harlem. It turned out this woman was with the Society for the Prevention of Cruelty to Children. She was going to put me in the shelter they had, but it was too late already, the place was closed for the night. This turned out to be a break.

She took me and bought me dinner and then we went to a beautiful hotel where she got me a fine room with a bed all to myself. This place knocked me out. Years later I went back there to see the place and found it was only a YWCA – but it looked like the Waldorf Astoria then. This woman was so nice I tried to get her to give me a job.

'I'll work for you hard,' I told her. 'I'll clean your house, wash your steps, scrub your floors.' But then she'd ask me my name and I still wouldn't tell her. She was wise to me. She'd smile when I refused to tell her my name. 'I know you,' she'd tell me. 'You're smart.'

The next morning she came and took me to the home run by the Society. It was nice there. The food was good. There were plenty of kids around and nothing to do but play. There was a huge playground out back, with slides and swings and things, screened at the sides and the top.

I must have stayed there a couple of weeks before Mom found out where they had me. They took me downstairs one morning to meet the lady who had come to pick me up. It wasn't my mother, though. It was a woman by the name of Mrs Levy.

'I'm not going with you,' I told her right off. 'I'm staying.'

'Why?' she asked me. 'What's the matter?'

'Nothing,' I told her. 'I like this place.'

'But I came to take you to your mama,' she told me.

I noticed she didn't say 'mother' and she didn't say 'mammy.' She said 'mama.' And the way she said it kind of made me think I might take a chance. Mrs Levy was the lady from Long Branch Mom worked for. Mom was taking care of her kids, she told me, and she had drove down in her car to take me home with her.

When I heard she had a car, that settled it. And when I saw the pretty automobile, I was ready to go anywhere just for the ride. I hadn't been in a car so many times I could take a chance missing a ride. We drove from downtown New York to Long Branch.

Sadie and I were going to be together again at last. We were going to make it. She even had a job lined up for me – as a maid, naturally. What else?

The woman I was to work for was big, fat and lazy. She didn't do a thing all day except lay her big ass on the beach. I didn't do much more. All I had to do was sleep and eat, peel a few onions and vegetables to keep her hands pretty, wash a few dishes to keep them from getting rough, and dust a little so she wouldn't have to move around.

This great big greasy bitch didn't do a thing all day until about fifteen minutes before her old man was due home for dinner. Then she would kick up a storm. I didn't know my way around her fancy kind of joint. Instead of telling me what she wanted me to do, she'd get excited because her husband was waiting, start hollering at me and calling me 'nigger.' I had never heard that word before. I didn't know what it meant. But I could guess from the sound of her voice. It was weird, that house – filled with crazy furniture and junk that just collected dust – and pillows all over. How she used to dog me about those pillows!

It didn't last long. One day, just before she hauled off to the beach, she dragged out a big old blanket, threw it at me, and told me to wash it. I flipped. I wasn't supposed to do laundry, so I told her what she could do with her damn blanket. That was the end of that job. In the first place, I didn't want to be her maid, or anybody's. I figured there had to be something better than this.

When I went back to Mom's and told her what happened, she didn't know what the hell to do with me. She knew I'd never make it as a maid. I had finished the fifth grade in school in Baltimore and I hadn't been back. If I did go back, they might ask where the hell I had been. There was no place for me to go to school anyway, unless I had a place to live. Mom had a little money saved, and she finally said she'd take me to Harlem and board me out.

Mom wasn't really a square at all. Yet in many ways she was. The place she found for me to live was nothing less than a fancy apartment house off 141st Street in Harlem. People paid some high old rent there then. Mom got me a room in a beautiful apartment belonging to a lady named Florence Williams. I hadn't emptied basins, laid out Lifebuoy soap and towels in Alice Dean's place in Baltimore for nothing. I knew what was cooking. But Mom didn't. She paid my rent in advance to Florence, and with the straightest face in the world asked this handsome sharply dressed madam to take care of her little girl. Florence was one of the biggest madams in Harlem.

She might just as well have asked little Eleanora to take care of Florence. I thought I was a real hip kitty. In a matter of days I had my chance to become a strictly twenty-dollar call girl – and I took it. The Jelke stuff they made a big deal out of wasn't even new then. The only thing new about it – even to me – was the fancy telephone. I had seen those funny-looking telephones in the movies – the ones you answer lying in bed instead of the old-time wall jobs. From the moment I saw them I knew that was for me. Not just any kind, though. It had to be a white telephone. And that's what I had at Florence's place.

I soon had two young white cats to match I could depend on regular every week, one on Wednesday, one Saturday. Sometimes one of them would make it twice a week. The madam took five out of every twenty dollars for the rent. This still left me more than I could make in a damn month as a maid. And I had someone doing *my* laundry. It was a small place. Florence only had two other girls, a yellow one named Gladys and a white girl whose name I don't remember.

It wasn't long before I had money to buy a few things I'd always wanted – my first honest-to-God silk dress and a pair of spike-heeled ten-dollar patent-leather pumps.

But I didn't have what it took to be a call girl. In the first place, and for damn good reason, I was scared to death of sex. First there had been the deal with Mr Dick. Then when I was twelve a trumpet player from a big Negro orchestra had had me for the first time on the floor of my grandmother's parlor. That was rugged enough to finish me with men for a while. I remember being hurt so, I thought I was going to die. I went to Mom, took my bloody clothes and threw them down in disgust.

'So this is what you and Pop used to do when I slept at the foot of your bed in a cedar chest,' I screamed at her.

What could she say? Nothing. She moaned a little about her baby having had a man and she worried herself half to death for days for fear I would have a baby the way she had had me. I had hit her where she couldn't hit back. I swore then I was through with men and I told her she needn't worry any more about me doing what she and Pop had done.

Then one day at Florence's place a big Negro had come in and insisted on having nobody but me. He gave me fifty dollars. He should have. It was a small price to pay for nearly killing me. I was out of commission for days and couldn't even put my two feet on the floor. Mom came to see me during that time and found me sick in bed. She didn't know what had been going on, but after one look at me she said she was taking me to the hospital.

I was so sick I didn't care if I went – until I saw the letters on the cap of the cat who came with the ambulance cart. I had heard about that hospital he came from. Girls I knew went there with pneumonia and came out without any ovaries. So I sat right up in bed, sent the ambulance away, crawled to the bathroom, had something to eat later, and I was all right.

No wonder I was scared to death of sex. And no wonder I did what I did when a Negro cat came around by the name of Big Blue Rainier. He was with Bub Hewlett, who was running Harlem in those days. Both of them are dead now, but they were big men then.

I went to jail for refusing to go to bed with Blue. I tried to tell him it wasn't anything personal, I just wasn't going to bed with any more Negroes.

With my regular white customers, it was a cinch. They had wives and kids to go home to. When they came to see me it was wham, bang, they gave me the money and were gone. I made all the loot I needed. But Negroes would keep you up all the damn night, handing you that stuff about 'Is it good, baby?' and 'Don't you want to be my old lady?'

Talk about women getting salty when they get scorned! You should have seen Big Blue.

'What the hell good is she?' he hollered at Florence. 'She's the only colored girl in the house and she won't take Negroes?' Florence was a fine woman, but it would have been worth her life to stick up for me.

Blue knew I was a baby, but he had me busted just the same. He and Bub were real tight with the cops. The next morning I was in the kitchen with the other girls having breakfast when the cops broke in. They had stool-pigeon witnesses with them who screamed at me. 'That's her,' they said, pointing at me. 'That's her.'

So they hauled me off to jail, not for anything I did, but for something I wouldn't do. Those were rotten days. Women like Mom who worked as maids, cleaned office buildings, were picked up on the street on their way home from work and charged with prostitution. If they could pay, they got off. If they couldn't they went to court, where it was the word of some dirty grafting cop against theirs.

They booked me and hustled me off to the Jefferson Market Court. The place was full of what they called 'wayward women' in those days, and of course the vice squad fuzz. When I saw who was on the bench I knew I was cooked. It was Magistrate Jean Hortense Norris, the first woman police judge in New York, a tough hard-faced old dame with hair bobbed almost like a man's.

She had made a big name for herself, running around making sweet talk about how it took a woman to understand social problems. But I had heard from the girls who had been in her court that this was all a lot of crud. She was tougher than any judge I ever saw in pants before or since. If the girls had lawyers, they'd move heaven and earth to get their cases put off to some other judge.

I knew if you pleaded guilty you caught hell. If you pleaded not guilty, you might even get worse. I didn't have anybody to get me a lawyer, not that it would have done much good. If that judge had guessed for a minute I was only fifteen she would probably have packed me off to Bedford Reformatory until I was twenty-one.

But Mom came down to court and stopped that. She swore on a stack of Bibles I was eighteen. If they had checked up on her, it would have showed Mom had given birth to me when she was nine. But they didn't. It cost Mom a lot to tell a lie like that. She couldn't stand lying and made me the same way. She never lied unless she had to save somebody's life. And neither did I.

When my case came up, the judge picked up a piece of paper, read it off, said it was a health report that I was sick. This was pretty funny because they hadn't tested me for anything; there hadn't been time. Besides, I was clean, I knew I was clean, and the tests proved it later.

But this old girl judge didn't believe me. She read her lecture about how young I was, and how sick, and said she was going to be lenient with me and send me to a city hospital in Brooklyn. They hustled me out the way they had hustled me in. And that was that.

At the hospital they were giving everybody shots of salvarsan for syphilis – only it was called 'bad blood' then. I didn't get any shots, I gave them. I worked with the doctors and saw girls coming in with their arms eaten up from big round sores where somebody missed a vein and gave it to them in the muscle. Later I got promoted to the bismuth kick, where I used to give shots in the ass all by myself. I learned to handle those needles real good. All the girls used to ask for me because word got around that I never hurt anybody.

I might have done all my time at the hospital, but bad luck was dogging me. One night a big dike went after me. They call them lesbians now, but we just called them dikes. She tried to get at me. I took a poke at her, and down the stairs she went.

So they threw me out of the hospital after two weeks and I found myself back in the old Jefferson Market Court. The same court, the same judge, only this time she was really mad.

'I thought I was giving you a chance,' she spouted at me. 'But you turned out to be a girl of bad character.' Wham, bang, four months she handed me, and I was off to Welfare Island.

That place was filthy. Fifty girls were packed together in one awful ward, and some of them with TB. We got the kind of garbage to eat you wouldn't feed your dog. Every once in a while we'd all get put to work cleaning up the joint. That meant a bunch of social workers would come trooping through making an inspection. But after they'd leave, the rats would come out again and everything would slide back to filthy-dirty normal.

The rats in that place were bigger than anything I'd seen in Baltimore. And they all seemed like they'd been trained. They'd walk right past without bothering you unless they were hungry. And even if they were hungry they wouldn't bother the girls in the wards, they'd come in the kitchen just like a pet. I worked in the kitchen for a while, and there was one old rat, so beat up most of his fur was worn away, who used to come in regularly to get his chow.

All night I'd lay awake listening to the pleasure boats going by in the East River and wonder if I'd ever get out. Like everybody else, I was just counting the days. I was supposed to get fifteen days off for good behavior, which meant I had to count up to a hundred and five.

Then one day when I had the count down to seventy days to go, something happened that boosted my time back to eighty-five. There were plenty of dikes around that place too. And one of them had been dogging me. This day she made a pass at me, and I made a pass back with my fist. This little scuffle cost me my fifteen days off for good behavior and caused me to get tossed in the cooler.

That place was the end – a cell so tiny there wasn't room to take one step. You had a cot, room to stand up or sit down, and that was it. No lights, it was so dark down there you lost track of night and day and had to give up counting your time. After a while you didn't even care. They gave you two pieces of bread with saltpeter in it every day and some water. I had to do ten days on that diet, but I used to throw it back in their faces.

After you got out of the cooler you were punished by getting graduated to the laundry. The girls in the laundry used to holler at me, trying to buck me up.

'Stick it out,' they'd yell. 'Don't throw your food away. Eat it or you'll never make it out alive.'

I could hear their voices but I never got to lay eyes on a soul except the matron.

A dike was the cause of getting me in there, and another one was the cause of getting me out alive. This one matron was a chick who liked girls. I had said something to her the first time she came around and she thought I was cute. She used to sneak me a couple of cigarettes when I needed them bad, and I used to play along with her.

I knew she expected to get to make a pass at me when I got out. She expected me to be nice to her. So I didn't tell her any different.

She had her own reasons for being nice to me. But any kind of freakish feelings are better than no feelings at all. If that judge had only been a dike, she might have treated me like a piece of human flesh instead of a piece of evidence. If it hadn't been for this nice dikey matron, I don't know if I would have made it.

But one day they let me out and I graduated to the laundry. My last job there was a real break – I got to cook for the warden and his family. I used to make them crazy dishes I had learned from Mom – things she used to make for rich people, like chicken cacciatore with mushrooms and roast duck. This used to knock him out. When my time was running out, he made me an offer to stay on and cook for him.

'You come to my house and I'll cook for you,' I told him. 'I'm never coming back here.'

My job cooking for the warden made me a big shot in the joint. As a privileged character, I got to sleep in the bed by the window in the ward. Also, it meant I got out on time. They couldn't keep books on the island. Girls that were supposed to do three years sometimes did three or four weeks extra because some bookkeeper goofed. Then one day they'd discover some girl still there who was supposed to be out. They'd ask her what she thought she was doing. 'You were supposed to be out weeks ago,' they told one girl.

But I got out right on the nose at the end of four months. It was summer when I went in, without a stitch to my name except my one and only silk dress and my spike-heeled patent-leather shoes. It was winter when they let me out, and when they checked me through the exit I got the dress, but the chick in the check room told me she couldn't find my shoes. I kicked up such a storm I thought they were going to keep me there. I raised so much hell the warden finally had to come down. When he found out what it was all about he said my shoes had to be there someplace. He gave orders for them to find them if they had to search the joint. The dame in the check room found them in a hurry. She handed them over – brand new and just her size.

So I got on that cold windy ferryboat to cross the East River in my spike shoes and my silk dress. But it hung on me like a prison uniform – I had dropped twenty-three pounds on the island.

When the boat hit the shore, it seemed like half the pimps in New York were there to meet us. They lined up at the docks to look us over. That's their business, that's where they auditioned their talent, and the cops did everything to make it easy, including directing the traffic. I must have looked sad, but there was a pimp there who gave me the 'Hi, baby', and asked me to go with him. He had a car waiting and wanted to take me to a house right off.

I had decided I was through with hustling, but I didn't tell him. And I had learned a lot on Welfare Island. I needed some clothes, especially a warm winter coat. And I needed them quick. He could get them for me. And he did.

I let him take me to a house and set me up. But I wouldn't give him any of my money. I was sending it all to Mom. When he found out, he flipped. I told him Mom was my pimp. He beat the hell out of me, and I had to hide out for a while.

So I went to Jamaica, Long Island. There I met Dorothy Glass. She had a big house out there where she ran poker games and other kinds of gambling. She was a real nice dame, the type of woman Mom thought Florence Williams was.

I stayed with her, waiting on tables and helping out to pay my way while I kept out of circulation. Once in a while I used to go to the Elks Club in Jamaica and sing. This way I could pick up a little change. But at Dorothy's place the toughest job I had was keeping her husband Lee out of my hair. By this time I could see trouble coming, so I quit when I was still ahead.

I used to tell people later about the tough time I'd had with Judge Jean Hortense Norris, but they just didn't believe it. I guess you have to live it before you can believe it.

Then in a few months everybody was talking about the judge I had been talking about. When the Seabury investigation hit the front pages in 1930–31, Judge Seabury himself took her to the Appellate Court, where he got her thrown off the bench by a unanimous vote, declaring her 'unfit' to be a judge.

This was the old dame that sent me to jail as a 'wayward woman'.

This was the character who told me I was a bad character. She should have gone to jail herself, but she never did. There were hundreds of girls that she had sent up, and a lot of them were waiting for her. If she had gone to jail I'd almost have been willing to do another short bit myself just to get my hands on her.

3

Painting the Town Red

By the time Mom and I had got together and found us a place of our own in Harlem the depression was on. At least, so we heard tell. A depression was nothing new to us, we'd always had it. The only thing new about it was the bread lines. And they were about the only thing we missed.

We moved into an apartment on 139th Street, and not long after, for the first time since I could remember, Mom was too sick to make Mass on Sunday. For her, that was really sick. Give her coffee every morning and Mass every Sunday, and she thought she could go on working forever. But she had to quit working out as a maid. She couldn't even walk, her stomach was so shot. She just had to stay put in bed.

What little money we had saved started running out and she was getting panicky. She had worked for most of her life, and it was beginning to tell on her. For almost half of that time she had been grieving over Pop. This didn't help any.

I had decided I was through turning tricks as a call girl. But I had also decided I wasn't going to be anybody's damn maid. The rent always seemed to be due, and it took some scuffling to keep from breaking my vows.

About that time Fletcher Henderson's band was working downtown at the Roseland Ballroom. It was the first Negro band to work there, and Pop Holiday was with them on the guitar. Sick as she was, Mom was too proud to turn to Pop and ask his help with the rent money. But not me.

I used to go right down there and haunt him. Pop was in his early thirties then, but he didn't want anyone to guess it – especially the young chicks who used to hang around the entrance waiting for the musicians.

I was around fifteen then, but I looked plenty old enough to vote. I used to wait for him down in the hallway. I'd try to catch his eye and call out to him, 'Hey, Daddy.' I soon found out just waving at him would make him feel like forty-five, and he didn't like that. He used to plead with me.

'Please,' he'd say, 'whatever you do, don't call me Daddy in front of these people.'

'I'm going to call you Daddy all night unless you give me some damn money for rent,' I'd tell him. That would do it.

I'd take the money home to Mom, proud as all get out. But I couldn't hurt her feelings by telling her where it came from. If she kept worrying me about it, I'd finally tell her I stole it. Then we'd have a fight and she'd tell me I was going to end up in jail again.

One day when the rent was overdue, she got a notice that the law was going to put us out on the street. It was in the dead cold of winter and she couldn't even walk.

I didn't know they did things like that up North. Bad as it was down South, they never put you out on the street. When we were due to get set out on the street the next morning, I told Mom I would steal or murder or do anything before I'd let them pull that. It was cold as all hell that night, and I walked out without any kind of coat.

I walked down Seventh Avenue from 139th Street to 133rd Street, busting in every joint trying to find a job. In those days 133rd Street was the real swing street, like 52nd Street later tried to be. It was jumping with after-hours spots, regular hour joints, restaurants, cafés, a dozen to a block.

Finally, when I got to Pod's and Jerry's, I was desperate. I went in and asked for the boss. I think I talked to Jerry. I told him I was a dancer and I wanted to try out. I knew exactly two steps, the time step and the crossover. I didn't even know the word 'audition' existed, but that was what I wanted.

So Jerry sent me over to the piano player and told me to dance. I started, and it was pitiful. I did my two steps over and over until he barked at me and told me to quit wasting his time.

They were going to throw me out on my ear, but I kept begging for the job. Finally the piano player took pity on me. He squashed out his cigarette, looked up at me, and said, 'Girl, can you sing?'

I said, 'Sure I can sing, what good is that?' I had been singing all my life, but I enjoyed it too much to think I could make any real money at it. Besides, those were the days of the Cotton Club and all those glamour pusses who didn't do nothing but look pretty, shake a little, and take money off tables.

I thought that was the only way to make money, and I needed forty-five bucks by morning to keep Mom from getting set out in the street. Singers were never heard of then, unless it was Paul Robeson, Julian Bledsoe, or someone legit like that.

So I asked him to play 'Trav'lin' All Alone.' That came closer than anything to the way I felt. And some part of it must have come across. The whole joint quieted down. If someone had dropped a pin, it would have sounded like a bomb. When I finished, everybody in the joint was crying in their beer, and I picked thirty-eight bucks up off the floor. When I left the joint that night I split with the piano player and still took home fifty-seven dollars.

I went out and bought a whole chicken and some baked beans – Mom loved baked beans – and raced up Seventh Avenue to the house. When I showed Mom the money for the rent and told her I had a regular job singing for eighteen dollars a week, she could hardly believe it.

As soon as she could get out of bed she came down to see for herself and became my biggest booster. In those days they had five or six singers in the clubs and they called them 'ups.' One girl would be 'up' and she would go from table to table singing. Then the next one would be 'up' and she'd take over. I was an 'up' from midnight every night until the tips started thinning out, maybe around three o'clock the next morning.

In those days, too, all the girls took money off the tables, but I broke that up. With my first loot I got me a pair of fancy drawers with little rhinestones on them. But I didn't like the idea of showing my body. There was nothing wrong with my body, I just didn't like the idea. When the time came to take those bills off the table, I was always messing up.

One night a millionaire came in the joint and put out a twenty-dollar bill on the table. I wanted that twenty-dollar bill so bad. I really tried, but I dropped it so many times he got disgusted and said, 'Why, you're nothing but a punk kid. Get the hell away from here.'

When I finished my 'up' he must have felt sorry for me. Anyway, he asked me to come back and have a drink with him. When I did, he gave me the twenty-dollar bill in my hand. I figured, if a millionaire could give me money that way, everybody could. So from then on I wouldn't take money off tables. When I came to work the other girls used to razz me, call me 'Duchess' and say, 'Look at her, she thinks she's a lady.'

I hadn't got my title Lady Day yet, but that was the beginning of people calling me 'Lady.'

When Mom came to hear me sing and I started to make the rounds, I would always start at her table. After I'd made five or six bucks in tips I'd split with the piano player and give the rest to Mom to hold. The first night I did this she decided she'd get into the act and do a little shilling. The next time around she made like a big shot and started the ball rolling by handing me a big tip – two or three bucks of my own money. I'd throw it in with the rest, and when I finished the round I'd split with the piano player again. She got me so mixed up, acting like a duchess and handing me my own money, I got into a helluva rassle with the piano player.

When it came time to settle up for the night I tried to get back the money that belonged to me. I had given it to Mom and she had given it back, and this way I was splitting with the piano player three or four times. When I tried to explain this to him and told him my mother had done it, he looked at this young woman sitting at the table and flipped.

'Bitch,' he said, 'that's not your mother.' There was a real hassle before I could convince him Mom was really my mother, and only trying to help. Later on I got Mom a job in the kitchen at the Log Cabin. We had the joint sewed.

Prohibition was on its last legs then. And so were the blind pigs, the cribs and club and after-hours joints that Prohibition set up in business. Some people thought it would go on like that forever. But you can call the roll of the wonderful joints that thrived before repeal in 1933 – they're mostly memories now: Basement Brownies, the Yea Man, the Alhambra, Mexico, the Next, the Clam House, the Shim Sham, the Covan, the Morocco, the Spider Web.

Every night the limousines would wheel uptown. The minks and ermines would climb over one another to be the first one through the coalbins or over the garbage pails into the newest spot that was 'the place.'

Everything started for me there at the Log Cabin. A lot of big people used to come around. One night the boss introduced me to Paul Muni, who was standing at the bar. Another time John Hammond, who was on his way to becoming a big man in the music business, came in. The next time he brought Mildred Bailey, Red Norvo, and a young, serious, good-looking fellow named Benny Goodman. Mildred was the famous Rocking Chair Lady. Red was a well-known musician and Mildred's husband. And Benny was a radio-studio musician who talked a lot then about having his own band one day. They used to come around often. One night Mildred slapped Red Norvo's face and walked out of the place. They told me she was jealous of me and Red. But I didn't even know he had noticed me.

By then Bobby Henderson was playing piano for me. I still think he was the greatest.

Another time John Hammond brought in Joe Glaser, the big agent and manager. He was handling Louis Armstrong, Mildred Bailey, and practically everybody who got to be anybody. Glaser signed me up on the spot.

Then I started moving from club to club in Harlem. And everywhere I went something was happening. Of all the big people who came up to hear me sing, I think I liked Bernie Hanighen the best. He was a famous song writer. I loved his songs and I loved him. I used to feature 'When a Woman Loves a Man' and 'When the Moon Turns Green,' both his tunes. Bernie used to stay in a joint for hours, listening to me sing and giving me big tips when I did his tunes. But for him I'd have gladly sung anything for nothing. I loved that guy.

Benny Goodman came around plenty, too, and eventually he asked me to make my first record with him. I'll never forget it. Benny came up to get me and took me to the studio downtown. When we got there and I saw this big old microphone, it scared me half to death. I'd never sung in one and I was afraid of it. Nobody was wise to how scared I was except Buck, of the famous team of Buck and Bubbles, who was around for that session. Buck dug what was the matter with me and tried to snap me out of it.

'Don't let all these white folks see you scared,' he begged me. 'They'll be laughing at you.' He finally got me to stand near it, told me I didn't have to look at it or even sing into it, just stand near it. He was getting nowhere until he started to shame me, telling me I didn't have the nerve to go through with it.

That did it. I just ignored the thing and we did two tunes, 'Your Mother's Son-in-Law' and 'Riffin' the Scotch.' I got thirty-five bucks for the session, but nothing happened with the record.

Later on John Hammond paired me up with Teddy Wilson and his band for another record session. This time I got thirty bucks for making half a dozen sides, including 'I Only Have Eyes for You,' 'Miss Brown to You,' 'I Cover the Waterfront.' I didn't even know what royalties were in those days. I was glad to get the thirty bucks. I was billed as the vocalist with Teddy's band and that was all. But after a year or so, when the records started moving, I figured they were selling as much on the strength of my name getting known as Teddy's and I tried to get some more loot. But I couldn't.

It was then that Bernie Hanighen really went to bat for me. He had a job as a musical director at Columbia. They also put up records on the Vocalion label at thirty-five cents. Bernie pitched such a bitch up there at the office, he finally made them pay me seventy-five bucks for two sides. In those days you could take it or leave it. It didn't make any difference if the record companies made thousands off the records later, you'd never get another dime. This seventy-five bucks sometimes included tunes of my own that I had written. I got no royalties for them either.

Bernie almost lost his job at Columbia fighting for me. A lot of guys were big tippers uptown, but when it came to fighting for you downtown, they were nowhere. Not Bernie. He was the cause of me making my first records under my own name – not as anybody's damn vocalist, but as Billie Holiday period, and then the list of musicians backing me.

Bernie Hanighen is a great guy.

After the Log Cabin, I went on the bill at the Hotcha Club. And what a bill it was! They featured Billy Daniels, Jimmie Daniels, and me, with Bobby Evans as M.C. In between ups, on a little balcony on the second floor, there was Garland Wilson at the piano for intermission. It would take quite a few thousand a week to pull together a show like that today. But in those days it was all thrown in with a dollar dinner. And people used to come up there for the food, too. The chicken cacciatore was one of the attractions. While waiting for it, they would get me. It was still a while before it was the other way around.

Then people started coming back to hear me. Franchot Tone and his lovely mother used to come to every place I ever worked, from Pod's and Jerry's to Dickie Wells's. Mrs Tone was crazy about me and she loved Billy Heywood and Cliff Allen, who had a great act at the Basement Brownies. At the Hotcha I met Ralph Cooper. He was a big shot who'd been in the movies already and he used to tell Frank Schiffman, who ran the Lafayette Theatre and the Apollo, who to hire. Ralph convinced Schiffman to come and catch me. When Schiffman asked Cooper what style I had, Cooper was stumped.

'You never heard singing so slow, so lazy, with such a drawl,' he told him. But he still couldn't put any label on me.

This, I always figured, was the biggest compliment they could pay me. Before anybody could compare me with other singers, they were comparing other singers with me.

'It ain't the blues,' was all Cooper could tell him. 'I don't know what it is, but you got to hear her.'

So Schiffman came up. After he heard me he offered to put me on the bill at the Apollo for fifty a week. This was something in those days. Uptown, the Apollo was what the Palace was downtown.

Unless it was the records of Bessie Smith and Louis Armstrong I heard as a kid, I don't know of anybody who actually influenced my singing, then or now. I always wanted Bessie's big sound and Pops' feeling. Young kids always ask me what my style is derived from and how it evolved and all that. What can I tell them? If you find a tune and it's got something to do with you, you don't have to evolve anything. You just feel it, and when you sing it other people can feel something too. With me, it's got nothing to do with working or arranging or rehearsing. Give me a song I can feel, and it's never work. There are a few songs I feel so much I can't stand to sing them, but that's something else again.

If I had to sing 'Doggie in the Window,' that would actually be work. But singing songs like 'The Man I Love' or 'Porgy' is no more work than sitting down and eating Chinese roast duck, and I love roast duck. I've lived songs like that. When I sing them I live them again and I love them.

The morning I opened at the Apollo I had been up all night singing at the Hotcha and went direct from there to the theatre. The show was scheduled to go on at 10 AM, and by the time I was up I had gone to the bathroom eighteen times. Pigmeat Markham, the comedian, was on the same bill and he saved my life. They were playing the introduction and he was standing in the wings. At the last moment I grabbed and told him to do something because I had to split for the bathroom again.

'It's no bathroom for you, girl,' Pigmeat said. 'You're going on stage.' He saw I was scared, so he just grabbed me and gave me a big old healthy shove. When I stopped I was halfway across the stage. I got to the mike somehow and grabbed it. I had a cheap white satin dress on and my knees were shaking so bad the people didn't know whether I was going to dance or sing. Even after I opened my mouth they weren't sure. One little broad in the front row hollered out, 'Look, she's dancing and singing at the same time.'

I opened with Bernie Hanighen's song, 'If the Moon Turns Green.' By the time I went into 'The Man I Love' I was all right. Then the house broke up. There's nothing like an audience at the Apollo. They were wide awake early in the morning. They didn't ask me what my style was, who I was, how I had evolved, where I'd come from, who influenced me, or anything. They just broke the house up. And they kept right on doing it. I played the Apollo for the second week. This was one of the few times it happened there, if I do say so myself. And I damn well do.

Of all those nights in all those spots in Harlem, the one I remember best was a rough night at the Hotcha. I was walking by the bar when I spotted a young, handsome cat sitting there fast asleep. While I was keeping an eye on him, I saw a whore getting ready to clip his wallet out of his back pocket. I told that broad to leave him alone.

'What do you care?' she said. 'I'll split the loot with you.'

'No you won't,' I said. 'He's my old man.'

He was no such thing, of course, but what did she know? She gave the wallet to me and I gave it back to him. And that's the way I met Louis McKay. One time when he was real sick I took him home to our place and Mom nursed him back into shape. We went around together for quite a while.

Later, it was sometimes years between the times I saw him again. He went his way and I went mine. But when I told that broad he was my man, I thought I was lying. Later it turned out I had been speaking the truth and didn't know it.

4

If My Heart Could Only Talk

My great-grandmother was a white man's mistress, doxy, common-law wife, whatever you want to call it. She was also just a slave on his plantation. Bad as things were in those days, black people and white people at least lived in the same world. The white people made it – built the quarters, decided who'd work in the fields, who'd pick cotton, and who'd squeeze mint in the big house. They decided who got what to eat, who got bought, and who got sold.

The white women didn't have as much to do with it as the men. But they only had to look out their windows to see what was going on. There was damn little 'segregation' on the plantations in the daytime, even less at night. Many a night my white great-grandfather went out in back of the little house where my great-grandmother lived – with her kids and his. He didn't need any social worker to tell him about 'conditions.' He knew what it was like back there.

In the early thirties when Mom and I started trying to kick and scratch out a living in Harlem, the world we lived in was still one that white people made. But it had become a world they damn near never saw. Sure, some of them patronized the after-hours joints; they came to the Cotton Club – a place Negroes never saw inside unless they played music or did the shakes or shimmies. But these were just side shows specially set up for white folks to come and pay their money for kicks.

These places weren't for real. The life we lived was. But it was all backstage, and damn few white folks ever got to see it. When they did, they might as well have dropped in from another planet. Everything about it seemed to be news to them.

It was rugged. Sometimes I wonder how we survived. But we

did. If we didn't have what it took at the beginning, we picked it up along the way.

Our little flat was more than a home. It was a combination YMCA, boardinghouse for broke musicians, soup kitchen for anyone with a hard-luck story, community center, and after-after-hours joint where a couple of bucks would get you a shot of whisky and the most fabulous fried-chicken breakfast, lunch, or dinner anywhere in town.

Mom just loved people. Part of this might have come from never wanting to be alone, where she could only brood over Pop. Part of it must have come from her fears for me. She knew she wouldn't be around for very long to take care of me. There was damn little she could do to protect me after she was gone. All she had was me. All I had was her. She always figured if she was good to people and did things for them without any reward on this earth she was laying up good will in some heavenly bank. Then after she was gone I'd have something to draw on. And some of these people, she hoped, would be good to me in return. It hasn't worked that way. Not yet anyway. But that's the way she felt, bless her.

Mom not only loved people, she believed in them. She believed God made them, so there had to be some good in everybody. She found good in the strangest places and in the strangest people. She could find good in pimps and whores, even in thieves and murderers.

A bitch might be turning fifteen tricks a day and come to Mom in trouble, and Mom would go to bat for her, saying, 'She's a good little thing deep down underneath, and that's what matters.'

She'd have a fit if someone dropped their hat on the bed or dropped salt on the floor. These were things she really took seriously. But she wouldn't bat an eye at the other things people did. She kept her eye on the good spots she found in them somewhere.

You could be the biggest thief and scoundrel on the face of the earth, but all you had to do was tell Mom you were a musician and give her a little story and she'd give you everything in the house that wasn't nailed down.

People took advantage of her, sure. But there wasn't a cat around in those days who didn't respect her. If Mom caught herself saying 'goddamn' she'd have to go confess it. She was that proper and respectable. The house might be full and she'd be fixing fried chicken for a party of characters, and a fracas would start – some cat would be cussing out some broad a blue streak. But he'd always stop somewhere in the middle, out of respect to Mom, and say, 'Excuse me, Mom, I'm sorry, but I got to straighten this whore out.'

I never got beyond the fifth grade in school – and they were Baltimore's broken-down segregated schools at that. But I guess you could call that progress. Mom was only thirteen years older than me and had never got to school at all.

In my time the Board of Education didn't care enough about it to send some social worker chasing after me. In Mom's time they didn't care at all.

One of the things we did together in those early Harlem days was hold classes. I was the teacher, Mom the pupil. And I taught her to read and write. Nothing I ever did gave me such a kick as getting a handwritten note from her later when I was on the road, or watching her fall out when she read a letter from Louis Armstrong signed 'Red Beans and Ricely Yours.'

In between the time I got off Welfare Island and started singing around Harlem, I must have spent six months doing nothing. This drove Mom crazy. When she used to heckle me, I used to heckle back. 'I ain't in jail,' I'd tell her; 'I ain't disgracing nobody.' I had a little loot and I wasn't going to do nothing until it was gone.

One day, in order to break up this same old argument, I was taking Mom to the old Lafayette Theatre in Harlem. Louis Armstrong was playing there and Mom was crazy about him.

We were crossing Seventh Avenue when a cat I knew hollered at me.

'Girl,' he said, 'come *here*. Jimmy's got the best panatella you ever smoked in your life.'

I tried to brush him off, but he wouldn't brush.

I tried to shove him away like I'd never seen him before and at the same time give him a sign to shut up, I wasn't alone.

He kept right on. 'That's all right,' he said. 'Who's she? Your sister? Bring her along too. There'll be blue lights and red lights and we'll pitch a ball.'

Mom knew about reefers, but she didn't know I'd been smoking them for a year. She flipped. 'You get out of here,' she told our friend. 'If you don't, I'm going to put her away until she's twenty-one, and you in jail.'

We never got to see a movie, or Louis Armstrong, or nothing that day. When we got home I told Mom I had been smoking reefers for a year.

'If you'd seen any change in me,' I tried to tell her, 'you'd have sure let me know about it. And you didn't. So doesn't that prove that smoking reefers has done me no harm?'

She didn't want to listen, but she had to.

I tried to tell her they hadn't done me any harm. It was just shock she got from finding it out this way that had made her angry. But she had been taken in by the stuff she'd read and heard about what marijuana does to you. She'd believe that before she'd believe her own eyes. She thought I was headed for trouble and that it was my fault because I was weak.

The first time Pop heard me sing as the main attraction in a Harlem joint it turned into a big scene too. Mom was there that night, sitting at another table. She never drank a drop, but this night she broke her rule. I guess she always resented people jumping to the conclusion that my musical talent all came from the Holiday side of the family.

Duke Ellington had just written 'Solitude' along about then, and after three drinks Mom stood up in this joint on 139th Street, said something about Billie not being the only star in the family, and then started singing 'Solitude' in her tinny, high, baby voice. She sounded like Butterfly McQueen singing out of her register, but she stuck it out for one whole chorus until the whole joint was listening – even Pop.

Pop had been sitting across the room with his new wife, Fanny, but after Mom did this number he came over and sat down with Mom. Mom smiled at him like he was the only man in the world. And Pop was very nice.

'Eleanora's going to be a big star in show business, isn't she?' said Pop to Mom.

Mom beamed with pride and love all mixed up together. 'She's a big star already,' she said.

Those smiles bouncing back and forth between them must have bugged Fanny Holiday no end. She flipped and came bustling across the room and hit Mom over the head with her pocketbook. When Fanny landed her first blow on Mom, I got into it and started whaling away at Fanny. Pop tried to untangle us, but we were too much for him. Big Sid Catlett, the bigtime drummer, was there and tried to get us apart. But we were too much for him. He came over, told us the police were on the way, and then threw me and Mom into a cab and sent us home.

In those days everything that happened, happened at a jam session somewhere. I'll never forget the night Benny Goodman brought a skinny young cat uptown with him by the name of Harry James. It was one of the nights almost everybody was on deck – Roy Eldridge, Charlie Shavers, Lester Young, Benny Webster.

James was pretty hostile at first, as I remember him. He came from Texas, where Negroes are looked on like they're dirt. It showed. We had to break him out of that – and also of the idea that he was the world's greatest trumpet player. Buck Clayton, whom I thought was the prettiest man I'd ever seen, was a big help. He blew him out with his horn. Of all the cats around, Buck played a style that was sweeter than the others and closer to the thing Harry James was trying to do. It only took a few earfuls of Buck Clayton's playing, and Harry wasn't so uppity. He'd had his lesson, and after that he came up to jam and loved it.

It was at one of these sessions I first met Lester Young. From then on Lester knew how I used to love to have him come around and blow pretty solos behind me. So whenever he could, he'd come by the joints where I was singing, to hear me or sit in. I'll never forget the night Lester took on Chu Berry, who was considered the greatest in those days. Cab Calloway's was the biggest band and Chu Berry's was one of its big sounds.

Well, this night Benny Carter was jamming for a session with

Bobby Henderson, my accompanist. And then there was Lester with his little old saxophone held together with adhesive tape and rubber bands. Chu was sitting there and everybody started arguing as to who could blow out whom, trying to promote a competition between Lester and Chu.

Benny Carter knew Lester could shine in this sort of duel, but for everybody else the end of the story was considered a pushover: Chu was supposed to blow Lester right out of the place. Chu had this big pretty gold horn, but he didn't have it with him. Benny Carter wouldn't let that stop him. He was like me, he had faith in Lester. So he volunteered to go and pick up Chu's horn. He did and came back.

And then Chu Berry made the same mistake Sarah Vaughan was later to make with me. He suggested they do 'I Got Rhythm,' just the way Sarah had suggested 'I Cried for You.' Anything but that! 'I Cried' was my damn meat, just like 'Rhythm' was Lester's.

He blew at least fifteen pretty choruses, none of them the same, and each one prettier than the last. When the fifteenth one was down, Chu Berry was finished, just like Sarah was finished after my eighth chorus of 'Cried.'

Chu's gang were die-hards, and they were sick. All they could say to console themselves was that Chu had a bigger tone. What the hell that meant, I'll never know. What difference how big a tone is or how small, as long as Lester's line was moving in that wonderful way, with those chords, changes and those notes that would positively flip you with surprise? Chu was a mature man with a great big growl. Lester was a young man. There ain't no rule saying everybody's got to deliver the same damn volume or tone.

But anyway, this talk about a big tone messed with Lester for months. And me too. So I said, 'What the hell, Lester, don't let them make a fool of us. We'll get you a big horn with big fat reeds and things and no damn rubber bands around it holding you back. We'll get us a tone.'

So every time Lester could get a dime together he'd get him some more reeds and start cutting them up all kinds of different ways. He got him a new horn, too, and thought that would end him up with a big fat growl. But his tone never got any bigger. He wasn't meant to sound like Chu and he soon gave up trying.

Everyone's got to be different. You can't copy anybody and end up with anything. If you copy, it means you're working without any real feeling. And without feeling, whatever you do amounts to nothing.

No two people on earth are alike, and it's got to be that way in music or it isn't music.

I never forget this wonderful old Spaniard, Pablo Casals, who played the cello once on TV. When he finished some Bach he was interviewed by some American chick. 'Every time you play it, it's different,' she gushed.

'It must be different,' said Casals. 'How can it be otherwise? Nature is so. And we are nature.'

So there you are. You can't even be like you once were yourself, let alone like somebody else.

I can't stand to sing the same song the same way two nights in succession, let alone two years or ten years. If you can, then it ain't music, it's close-order drill or exercise or yodeling or something, not music.

Early one morning, after one of these jam sessions folded, Lester went back to Mom's with me to get some of her early breakfast specials. He had been living at a well-known Harlem hotel, and he was almost a nervous wreck from *that*. A few mornings before, he had opened his dresser drawer and found an unregistered guest staring him in the face. A big dirty old rat the size of my dog was using his shirts for a pad.

He got someone to help him and they carried the dresser down to the lobby. Everybody got brooms and sticks and mops and things. They wanted to let that rat out, then corner him and leave the evidence at the desk. If he had complained to the management and didn't have the proof by the tail, they were sure to accuse him of smoking somebody's bushes.

So Lester and the broom brigade all came to attention, someone opened the drawer, there was a great swinging of weapons, but the damn rat slipped by all of them and got away.

That left Lester shaky enough. Then one night Hal West, the drummer who worked in a trio with him, was putting some straightener on his hair. That stuff they peddled then would burn you like crazy unless you were careful and had plenty of water to put on after. Just as Hal got it on his hair, he turned on the water faucet and nothing happened. His head was burning up, as he tried one faucet, then the other, and got nothing but gas. It burned him so, he finally had to stick his head in the toilet bowl to stop it.

Mom and I doubled up with laughter hearing Lester tell how dangerous it was for a young man living alone in a New York hotel. And when he said, 'Duchess, can I move in with you?' there was only one answer. Mom gave him a room and he moved in with us.

Ours was a big old railroad flat, two flights up, with two entrances off the hallway. The front door was my bedroom, with a door opening to the hall and a little room off it we used to call my playroom, where I kept my records and a beat-up old piano. In the back was the living room and Mom's room. In the middle, off the air shaft, were Lester's quarters.

It wasn't fancy, but it beat that damn hotel. And for Mom and me it was wonderful having a gentleman around the house. Lester was always that.

Lester was the first to call Mom 'Duchess' – and it turned out to be the title she carried to her grave. Lester and I will probably be buried, too, still wearing the names we hung on each other after he came to live with us.

Back at the Log Cabin the other girls used to try and mock me by calling me 'Lady,' because they thought I thought I was just too damn grand to take the damn customers' money off the tables. But the name Lady stuck long after everybody had forgotten where it had come from. Lester took it and coupled it with the Day out of Holiday and called me 'Lady Day.'

When it came to a name for Lester, I always felt he was the greatest, so his name had to be the greatest. In this country kings or counts or dukes don't amount to nothing. The greatest man around then was Franklin D. Roosevelt and he was the President. So I started calling him the President. It got shortened to Prez, but it still means what it was meant to mean – the top man in this country.

These jam sessions were really the thing. Every morning after I finished working there was always a big jam session on somewhere. Cats like Benny Goodman and Harry James would come up after they finished their gigs in the big radio studio orchestras. They would sit in with the greatest guys around – Roy Eldridge, Lester Young, Benny Webster. They were all friends of mine. But Benny Goodman was somebody special among the musicians I hung out with.

We'd get together once a week regularly at those jam sessions and spend a few hours together. This got to be a big deal mainly because my mother was so strict with me and didn't want me running around with white boys. And also Benny's sister Ethel was his manager then. She had eyes for Benny going to the top as a band leader, and she didn't want him to wreck his chances for making it by being seen with a little black chick.

But Benny was a nice cat, never a drag. And we used to outwit my mother and his sister in order to spend some time together.

This went on for a long time – right up to the time I fell in love, but good and hard, for the first time. It wasn't until that happened that I knew that what had gone on before was nothing but fooling around.

Sure, he was a musician too. He played piano – great piano. He played for me for a while. He was almost old enough to be my father. And he was married, and had two or three kids.

It was the first time I was ever wooed, courted, chased after. He made me feel like a woman. He was patient and loving; he knew what I was scared about, and he knew how to smooth my fears away.

But beyond that, no good could come of it. In fact, at one point I was taking it all so seriously it came mighty close to being tragic.

5

Getting Some Fun Out of Life

It wasn't long before I became a radio and movie actress on the side.
Shelton Brooks, the song writer, author of 'Some of These Days,'
had heard me sing. He was making a few bucks in radio and he
thought I could play some of the parts in a show he worked on. It
was one of those daytime soap-opera serials, *True Love Story* or *True
Romances* or something like that. Anyway, when you worked it was
in the mornings, so it didn't interfere with my night work. Shelton
was playing two or three parts on the same show. Sometimes
he'd be both the butler and the husband. So he fixed it up for me to
double as the wife and the maid. It was worth fifteen bucks a day
when you worked. And you know those serials about the troubles
of Mary could drag on and on. Those writers could make one little
quarrel last for weeks. For fifteen bucks a day this was a big deal.

Shelton must have been fifty then. That would make him older
than God by now. But they still don't come any sharper. He still plays
a great blues on the piano and he can make you laugh your sides apart.

With all this acting experience behind me, Shelton thought I
was ready for a crack at the movies. Not Hollywood, just Astoria,
Long Island. He got me a part out there playing mob scenes in a
picture with Paul Robeson. From that I got a real part in a short
featuring Duke Ellington. It was a musical, with a little story to it,
and it gave me a chance to sing a song – a real weird and pretty
blues number. That was the good thing about the part.

The rough part, of course, was that I had to play a chippie.
Opposite me there was a comedian who'll kill me because I can't
remember his name. He played my pimp or sweetheart. He was
supposed to knock me around.

He knocked me down about twenty times the first day of shooting. Each time I took a fall I landed on the hard old floor painted to look like sidewalk. And there was nothing to break my falls except the flesh on my bones. The second morning when I showed up at the studio I was so sore I couldn't even think about breaking my falls. I must have hit that hard painted pavement about fifty times before the man hollered 'Cut.'

I saw a little bit of this epic one time at the studio, but that was all. Mom, of course, thought I was going to be a big movie star and she told everybody to watch for the picture. I don't know if anybody else saw it, but we never did. It was just a short subject, something they filled in with when they couldn't get Mickey Mouse. We'd have had to hire a private detective to find out where the hell it was playing.

Most of the ofays, the white people, who came to Harlem those nights were looking for atmosphere. Damn few of them brought any along. One of them was a doll named Jimmy Donahue. Sure he was a millionaire, but he knew how to live. He didn't let his money drag him like some people do. He learned how to live it up. He knew how to get his kicks.

One night right after I closed in the early morning, I took Jimmy up to Small's after-hours joint. The place was jumping and it was just Jimmy's speed. He felt like he was home. He made a deal with the owner to close the place and he took over for a private party. He started hosting. He got into the act the first thing. And you've never seen anything like it before or since. When the chorus ponies got out on stage doing their stuff, Jimmy got right out there with them.

'Play the music,' he told the band.

Then he grabbed a big tablecloth, soaked it in champagne, and started swinging it around like a circus ringmaster at Madison Square Garden. While the band played 'I Can't Get Started,' Jimmy cracked that whip for two choruses. And that boy cracked it on beat, too. He flipped those little dancing girls around while the audience howled.

And he never hurt anybody. When he was through, he kissed all the girls, gave them fifty bucks apiece, and drank toasts to all of them with champagne.

Another thing about Jimmy, he didn't cut up that way and let his hair down only in front of Negroes because they weren't his equals or nothing like some cats did. No such rot. He acted the same way on his own home ground. I know. I saw him once when he put a dog of a party on its feet at Libby Holman's house in the East Fifties.

Libby's husband had been dead awhile and she was giving a party to celebrate her baby's birthday. She really did it up right. Benny Goodman's band was playing the Hotel Pennsylvania then. She hired the whole deal, Teddy Wilson, Gene Krupa, Lionel Hampton, Helen Ward, and me. Everybody was there. We all met them all. I remember Mrs Clark Gable was there, crying in her champagne. She had just broken up with Clark and he was about to marry Carole Lombard.

But things were just too hoity-toity. It wasn't getting going fast enough for Jimmy Donahue. I was talking with him. He was worried and figuring what he ought to do to help. Finally he thought of something and said, 'Watch me wake it up.'

'With what?' I said. 'We've been swinging, the band and me, for two hours. Everybody's drinking champagne, but nothing's happening. What do you think you're going to do?'

He didn't say a word. He walked out between two double doors that separated the two big living rooms. He stood there, cleared his throat, and said: 'Now, ladies and gentlemen, the party begins.'

Nobody paid him any mind, even when he followed the announcement by taking off his coat.

In a couple of minutes he came back, stood in the same place, and elaborately took off his shirt. Still nobody paid much attention.

But he didn't give up. Next time he did the same routine and took off his pants. Then he got a little attention. He kept on doing this slow elaborate strip, standing there between the double doors.

All of us broke up, and the party was on. Clifton Webb unloosed and started dancing. I've never seen a man dance like that. You'd have to have his money, I guess, to dance up on tables, chairs, sofas – everything but the walls and ceilings.

We had been hired to work for three hours, but it was nine the next morning before the ball was over. When Benny started rounding up his crew to take them home, we uncovered everybody but Lionel Hampton. Hamp couldn't be found. So the search was on. And where did we find him? All alone in a room upstairs, snoring up a breeze and cuddling a big-assed bottle of champagne.

His wife Gladys wanted to kill him. She had come with the group and sat outside in the car all night, waiting for him to finish the gig. Long before they made anything like the kind of money they have now, Gladys was a smart one. She watched Lionel's every move and planned the next one. She deserves plenty of credit for getting Hamp where he is now. I hope to see her get it.

They didn't have the price of a bottle of champagne between them then. But Gladys has two-hundred-dollar hats now. She's a hat freak, that girl. But she earned those bonnets the hard way.

Anyway, this was one hell of a party – the way a party's supposed to be. I'll never forget it or Jimmy. I wouldn't think of throwing a big ball unless I was sure Jimmy could come and keep things moving.

6

Things Are Looking Up

I joined Count Basie's band to make a little money and see the world. For almost two years I didn't see anything but the inside of a Blue Goose bus, and I never got to send home a quarter.

I had started at the Log Cabin for eighteen dollars a week. By the time I opened at Clarke Monroe's Uptown House I was getting thirty-five dollars – when I got it. Half the time Clarke would say he was short and come up with fifteen or twenty dollars. When I asked for the rest of my money he would start telling me how much I'd get from this one and that one in tips.

One night a man had given me fifty dollars in the joint for nothing at all, and Clarke would remind me of that every time I asked for the rest he owed me. I had spent some of my good loot trying to make the joint go. After my record with Teddy Wilson started moving I had a big cardboard sign painted with my picture on it for Clarke to put out front, to help bring people in. It began to be a drag – I was getting disgusted.

After I'd closed at the Apollo I was booked into a French joint in Montreal. This was my first date outside New York and I enjoyed it. I tasted champagne there for the first time – hated it and still do. But I like the people. I met a wonderful Canadian boy up there; he always used to tell me scotch would hurt my voice and try to get me on champagne. But I used to drink champagne with him at a table and then sneak into the kitchen for some scotch. He was a fine fellow, but his family caught onto what was going on and they broke it up but quick.

Anyway, John Hammond had brought the Basie band out of Kansas City and was backing their first tour. When they opened in

Pittsburgh, in the biggest hotel in town, they died like a dog – flopped. Hammond decided what they needed was a girl vocalist, so he put up some more financing, along with Willard Alexander of MCA, and asked me to join the band – at fourteen dollars a day.

I wasn't even getting my thirty-five dollars a week at the Uptown House, and I guess from one trip to Montreal I thought traveling would be one big romance like that, so fourteen dollars a day sounded real great.

Nobody bothered to tell me I'd have to travel five hundred to six hundred miles on a hot or cold raggedy-ass Blue Goose bus; that it would cost me two or three bucks a night for a room; that by the time I was through having my hair fixed and gowns pressed – to say nothing of paying for pretty clothes to wear – I'd end up with about a dollar and a half a day. Out of that I had to eat and drink and send home some loot to Mom.

Whenever I had a couple of bucks it was always so little I was ashamed to send it home, so I would give it to Lester Young to invest. I hoped he could shoot enough dice to parlay it into a bill big enough I didn't have to feel ashamed to send home.

The first time out we had been riding for three months, and neither Lester nor I had a dime. Both of us were actually hungry. Jimmy Rushing, the blues-singing 'Mr Five by Five,' was always the only one who had any loot. We went to him once and asked him real nice for a buck to buy a couple of hamburgers. He wouldn't give us nothing but a lecture on how he saved his money and how we petered ours away.

When we were on the bus coming back to New York from West Virginia, I couldn't stand the thought of coming home to Mom broke. I had four bucks when that crap game started on the bus floor.

'You're not shooting these four,' I told Lester. 'I'm shooting these myself.'

I got on my knees, and the first time up it was a seven. Everybody hollered at me that the bus had swerved and made me shoot it over.

Up came eleven. I picked up the four bucks right there and won the next three pots before someone said something about comfort.

I thought they said, 'What do you come for?' I said, 'I come for any damn thing you come for.' I didn't know the lingo, but I knew Lester did. So I told him I'd do the shooting and he could be the lookout man.

I was on my knees in the bottom of that bus from West Virginia to New York, a few hundred miles and about twelve hours. When we pulled up in front of the Woodside Hotel everybody was broke and crying. I was filthy dirty and had holes in the knees of my stockings, but I had sixteen hundred bucks and some change.

I gave some of the cats in the band enough loot to eat with and for car fare. But not Rushing. I didn't give him back a dime. I took what was left and split on uptown to Mom's. When I walked in she looked at me and like to died, I was so dirty and beat up. I just waited for her to say something, and she did.

'I'll bet you ain't got a dime, either,' Mom said.

I took that money, over a thousand dollars, and threw it on the floor. She salted a lot of it away and later it became the nest egg she used to start her own little restaurant, 'Mom Holiday's,' something she always wanted.

Basie did a wonderful job with the band, but he just wasn't his own boss. He was just out of Kansas City. A big booking agency was backing him and trying to sell the band. We'd play a whole string of riffraff joints, rough Negro dance halls in the South where people were sneaking in corn whisky from across the tracks, and then boom in the middle of this grind we would be booked into some white hotel.

We didn't have the right uniforms, clothes, equipment – the cats in the band didn't even have the right horns they needed – we'd all be beat from traveling thousands of miles with no sleep, no rehearsal, and no preparation – and yet we'd be expected to be real great.

After each crisis on the road we'd end up back in New York. Then there'd be a big strategy meeting, figuring what was wrong with straightening things out.

I was accused of romancing everyone in the band and this was leading to dissension. This was a damn lie and I said so. I wasn't doing anything with anybody in the band except one cat – and not very often with him at that.

The truth was, I was scared of the cats in the band because they were messing with too many chicks on the road.

Living on the road with a band, nobody had time to sleep alone, let alone with somebody. At night, as Lester used to say, we'd pull into a town, pay two to four bucks for a room, shave and take a long look at the bed, go play the gig, come back and look at the bed again, and then get on the bus. We got so fed up with it one time, Lester and me, we threatened to resign and ended up getting a raise. I got raised to fifteen a day and Lester got boosted to eighteen-fifty. I thought this was just too marvelous for words.

For my money Lester was the world's greatest. I loved his music, and some of my favorite recordings are the ones with Lester's pretty solos.

I remember how the late Herschel Evans used to hate me. Whenever Basie had an arranger work out something for me, I'd tell him I wanted Lester to solo behind me. That always made Herschel salty. It wasn't that I didn't love his playing. It was just that I liked Lester's more.

Lester sings with his horn; you listen to him and can almost hear the words. People think he's so cocky and secure, but you can hurt his feelings in two seconds. I know, because I found out once that I had. We've been hungry together, and I'll always love him and his horn.

I often think about how we used to record in those days. We'd get off a bus after a five-hundred-mile trip, go into the studio with no music, nothing to eat but coffee and sandwiches. Me and Lester would drink what we called top and bottom, half gin and half port wine.

I'd say, 'What'll we do, two-bar or four-bar intro?'

Somebody'd say make it four and a chorus – one, one and a half.

Then I'd say, 'You play behind me the first eight, Lester,' and then Harry Edison would come in or Buck Clayton and take the next eight bars. 'Jo, you just brush and don't hit the cymbals too much.'

Now with all their damn preparation, complicated arrangements, you've got to kiss everybody's behind to get ten minutes to do eight sides in.

When I did 'Night and Day' I had never seen that song before in my life. I don't read music, either. I just walked in, Teddy Wilson played it for me, and I did it.

With artists like Lester, Don Byas, Benny Carter, and Coleman Hawkins, something was always happening. No amount of preparation today is any match for them.

In the old days, if we were one side short on a date, someone would say, 'Try the blues in A flat,' and tell me, 'Go as far as you can go, honey.' I'd stand up there and make up my words as I went along.

Nowadays you have all this talk and bull and nothing's happening. On a recent date I tried to do it like the old days. I'd never seen the band or the arrangements, and I didn't know the songs they had picked for me, and they wanted me to do eight sides in three hours. We were doing all standards, but nobody could read the stuff; the drummer did nothing but sit there grinning; the music had wrong chords; everybody was squawking. We pushed out about nine sides like they wanted. But not a damn one of them was any good.

You can say what you want about the South, and I've said plenty. But when I've forgotten all the crummy things that happened down there in my days on the road, I'll still remember Fox Theatre in Detroit, Michigan. What Radio City is to New York, the Fox was to Detroit then. A booking there was a big deal. My salary went up automatically to three hundred dollars a week for the run of the show. Everybody was happy.

The show opened and closed with a line of chorus girls doing their bare-legged kicks like the Rockettes. In the middle the girls did a big pretty number, with lots of parading around, fancy costumes, lights, and what not.

But Detroit was between race riots then, and after three performances the first day, the theater management went crazy. They claimed they had so many complaints about all those Negro men up there on the stage with those bare-legged white girls, all hell cut loose backstage.

The next thing we knew, they revamped the whole show. They cut out the girls' middle number. And when the chorus line opened the show, they'd fitted them out with special black masks and mammy dresses. They did both their numbers in blackface and those damn mammy getups.

When he saw what was happening, Basie flipped. But there was nothing he could do. We had signed the contracts to appear, and we had no control over what the panicky theater managers did.

But that wasn't the worst of it. Next they told Basie I was too yellow to sing with all the black men in his band. Somebody might think I was white if the light didn't hit me just right. So they got special dark grease paint and told me to put it on.

It was my turn to flip. I said I wouldn't do it. But they had our name on the contracts, and if I refused it might have played hell with bookings, not just for me, but for the future of all the cats in the band.

So I had to be darkened down so the show could go on in dynamic-assed Detroit. It's like they say, there's no damn business like show business. You had to smile to keep from throwing up.

But after a few more months with more of the same I quit. Mother almost blew her top. She thought this was the biggest opportunity of my life and I was throwing it over.

After a few weeks I began to think she was right. It turned out to be almost six months before I did anything musical after I quit. I didn't even sing. I just ate my damn heart out.

There were a lot of great things about the Basie band, and the experts are just beginning to pick it to pieces after almost twenty years to find out what made it so great. But with the distance of years, you forget all the things that your nose used to be rubbed in, and can add up the score.

I still say the greatest thing about the Basie band of those days was that they never used a piece of music, still all sixteen of them could end up sounding like a great big wonderful one sound.

Most of my experience with bands before that had been in

hanging out with Benny Goodman. I used to listen to him rehearse with high-paid radio studio bands and his own groups. He always had big arrangements. He would spend a fortune on arrangements for a little dog-assed vocalist.

But with Basie, we had something no expensive arrangements could touch. The cats would come in, somebody would hum a tune. Then someone else would play it over on the piano once or twice. Then someone would set up a riff, a ba-deep, a ba-dop. Then Daddy Basie would two-finger it a little. And then things would start to happen.

Half the cats couldn't have read music if they'd had it. They didn't want to be bothered anyway. Maybe sometimes one cat would bring in a written arrangement and the others would run over it. But by the time Jack Wadlin, Skeet Henderson, Buck Clayton, Freddie Greene, and Basie were through running over it, taking off, changing it, the arrangement wouldn't be recognizable anyway.

I know that's the way we worked out 'Love of my Life' and 'Them There Eyes' for me. Everything that happened, happened by ear. For the two years I was with the band we had a book of a hundred songs, and every one of us carried every last damn note of them in our heads.

7

Good Morning, Heartache

I had been under contract to Joe Glaser for a year, but nothing was happening. Finally I got sore, went down to his office and raised hell.

It was then he told me he hadn't booked me anywhere because I was too fat. I told him to tell that to Mildred Bailey the Rocking Chair Lady. I was big, sure, but she still had plenty of pounds on me. But I started losing weight and finally he told me he had a job for me at the Grand Terrace Club in Chicago.

Mom and I both thought this was the start of something big. Mom was so proud that I was headlining, she was ready to give up everything to hit the road with me – our flat, everything.

We should have known better, but we didn't. The very first night, Ed Fox, the manager of the Terrace, started giving me a bad time. Fletcher Henderson's band was there. When I did my first number, 'If You Were Mine,' I knew that nobody understood my singing. They didn't like me; they didn't hate me either. They just didn't have any enthusiasm either way, like they hadn't been told by anybody yet whether I was good or bad. And when you're doing something new, you got to have somebody tell people. In those depression days when a club was paying an unknown singer seventy-five dollars a week, they expected people to go crazy. The manager got panicky and began to holler at me that I was stinking up his Grand Terrace, so why should he pay me seventy-five dollars a week?

When the Grand Terrace closed that first night, the manager was moaning and groaning so, you couldn't talk to him. Finally when he told me to get out of his office I said, 'Don't worry, I'm going.' But before I left I picked up an inkwell and bam, I threw it at him and threatened to kill him.

So there we were, Mom and I, stranded in Chicago without even a home to go back to, let alone any way of getting there. We finally found a friend who loaned us carfare.

Mom and I were licked. We came back on the bus to New York and exactly nothing.

Later, when I was a big star at Café Society Downtown, the panicky Ed Fox, manager of the Grand Terrace, came down with Joe Glaser. When he saw what happened there, he began to climb all over Glaser, trying to get me for the Grand Terrace.

'For Christsake,' Joe told him, 'don't you know who that is? That's the girl you threw out of the Grand Terrace, the one who threatened to kill you with an inkwell.'

He like to drop dead, but he still wanted to buy me. I told him and Joe the same thing. I wouldn't sing for him in the Grand Terrace again if I never sang anywhere.

I'll always remember the people who helped me on the way up, but I can't forget the others who went out of their way to give me a fast shove the other way. One day Joe Glaser told me to go down to Philadelphia for an audition at the Nixon Grand Theatre. It was to be a big chance on a big-time bill. Ethel Waters opened, Duke Ellington closed the show, and I was up for the soubrette spot. The Brown Sisters were also on the bill.

Once more Mom and I were sure I'd make it. Mom thought she knew Ethel Waters – she had worked for her in Philly for quite a while as a maid when she was a big star. Mom was sure this was my big chance, so she blew her whole week's salary to buy me an evening dress with shoes to match and stock arrangements of a couple of songs. This left just about enough for bus fare – one way – and something to eat. At the last minute I used the eating money to buy stage make-up. Then I went into the dime store and bought a tiny little satin handbag to match my dress.

I still remember that shaky moment I got up on the stage to audition. I told the piano player to give me 'Underneath the Harlem Moon,' which was real popular then. I hadn't finished the first chorus when Ethel Waters bounced up in the darkened theater.

'Nobody's going to sing on this goddamn stage,' she boomed, 'but Miss Ethel Waters and the Brown Sisters.'

That settled that. 'Underneath the Harlem Moon' was Miss Waters' big number. But nobody told me. I didn't have the faintest idea.

So the stage manager handed me two dollars and told me to get on the bus and go home. I threw the money at him and told him to kiss my ass and tell Miss Waters to do the same.

When I went out the stage door I didn't have a dime to my name. I stayed around Philly a couple of days before I could scuffle up enough to get back to New York on the bus and tell Mom what happened.

Later on Miss Waters was quoted as saying that I sang like 'my shoes were too tight.'

I don't know why Ethel Waters didn't like me. I never did a thing to her that I know of except sing her big number that day for my big Philly audition.

As I kept moving around and making the name Holiday a little famous round the country, I used to hear from Pop pretty regularly. He was so proud of me.

Then suddenly one night in February 1937, when I was working at the Uptown House, ten minutes before going on I was called to the phone. It was a long-distance call for me from Dallas, Texas.

A real cold voice said, 'Is this Eleanora Billie Holiday?'

I said yes.

'Is Clarence Holiday your father?'

I said yes again.

'He just died,' the voice said. He went on with some words I was too dazed to make out. 'You want to send for the body?'

I didn't know what to do or say. I stood there with the phone in my hand and couldn't say a word. Clarke Monroe, luckily, was nearby. He came to the phone. It was some veterans' hospital in Texas trying to weed out their morgue. Clarke was wonderful. He took over, loaned me his car, and took care of all the arrangements.

When his body arrived we found they had laid Pop out in his bandstand tuxedo. But his white dress shirt was covered with blood.

I never knew who to blame for that, but anyway Clarke got him straight before we let Mom in to see his body.

Mom walked up to Pop's coffin, and I can see her there now. She knelt there for four hours and twenty minutes. I know because I waited out every minute of it for her. She didn't shed a tear or make a sound. She just held her rosary in her hand, and if you looked closely you could see her lips move.

After a couple hours the man who ran the funeral parlor and I tried to get her up, but nobody could move her.

He was the only man she ever really loved. They hadn't been together for years, but that didn't ever change the way she felt about him. She felt he still belonged to her, or some part of him did, and she never got over his death.

She was very, very sentimental and just as religious. She could understand and forgive people who took marriage more lightly, but it was always a holy sacrament to her. A doctor had told her once when she was about to have the change of life that she should forget Pop and try to live normally and take a natural interest in some other man. But she wouldn't. He was her man.

People have really to feel deeply about something or somebody before a tragedy like Pop's death could turn into a comedy like his funeral.

The cast was not large, but it was crazy and complicated. First there was Mom and me. Then there was his second wife, Fanny Holiday, who was my stepmother. So I didn't have one crazy woman on my hands, I had two.

But that wasn't all. There were a few sporting girls claiming to be his one and only. But it wasn't long before I found out I had two stepmothers – the second one a white woman.

She showed up at Pop's coffin with two kids – my half brother and sister, who were white too. All this was news to me. But she was a lovely woman and the two kids were handsome. It turned out she was very wealthy, had met Pop when he worked at Roseland, and they had these two kids which she was raising as white.

Seeing my half sister and brother reminded me how crazy this country is. There was the Roseland management, the place where

I used to hang out in the downstairs hall and wait for Pop so I could bug him about the rent. Anybody who worked there and so much as looked at a white girl within sight of the management would lose his job in a minute. If they had caught Pop having a drink with a white bitch the management would have flipped.

But this was all for show, or it was for nothing. If they were trying to keep Negroes from sleeping with white girls, it sure worked in reverse. All the cops in the precinct couldn't have stopped if they tried. And here were the two kids to prove it.

I talked with her about the kids and about Pop. She told me she was bringing them up as white. I told her she could do as she damn well thought best, and if they could pass, let them. But I still thought she was wrong not to tell them the truth. They would catch on sometime – if they hadn't already, looking at their mother's face as she looked at Pop's body in that funeral parlor. Who did she think she was kidding? If I had been their age I'd have been wise the minute I walked in. And I wasn't putting those kids down as being a damn bit more stupid than me.

So getting together the funeral was a mess. The immediate family was to ride first. But deciding who was more immediate than whom was when the stuff hit the fan. And I caught it because I was running everything. The preacher, the doctor, the funeral director, all were asking me for their orders.

Naturally Mom said she was the one, the first, if not the only. So a big squabble started between her and Fanny Holiday. Mom put her foot down flatly and said if Fanny was going to ride in the first car she was riding somewhere else. I tried to referee by saying 'Liblab's dead, nobody can bring him back. He's going to be in the ground in about five damn minutes, and now what can you two women possibly have to fight about?' Liblab is the musician's word for ad lib, and that was Pop's nickname.

Mom was little Mrs Five by Five, but she was a proud one. She said she wouldn't ride with me and Fanny Holiday, and she kept her word. Clarke Monroe had loaned me his Cadillac, but Mom flew off and chartered a Cadillac of her own.

Fanny and I rode to the graveside together for the services.

There were cars of flowers and delegations from the Masons, the Elks, and Local 802, but there was no sign of Mom. It wasn't until I got back home that she finally rode up in her rented machine. She had gotten lost and couldn't find the cemetery.

Mom never really recovered from the shock of Pop's death. It took me a long time too. Especially a little while later when we finally learned how he had died. Big Sid Catlett had been in the room with him, in Don Redmond's band, and he told us what happened.

He had caught a funny kind of pneumonia. I suppose it would be simple now with penicillin and all. But then it was a big deal. He couldn't sleep, couldn't sit down, couldn't do anything except walk around town or pace the floor of his room.

And it wasn't the pneumonia that killed him, it was Dallas, Texas. That's where he was and where he walked around, going from hospital to hospital trying to get help. But none of them would even so much as take his temperature or take him in. That's the way it was.

Pop finally found a veterans' hospital, and because he had been in the Army, had ruined his lungs and had records to prove it, they finally let him in the Jim Crow ward down there.

By that time it was too late. He had a hemorrhage. All they could do for him was give him a bed to die in and notify his next of kin.

His death was an awful blow, but I kept right on singing after I heard about it. I don't know why. No one else understood either. I needed something to do. And I was sure Pop wouldn't have wanted me to stop on account of him or go in for any mourning or crying. For him, life had always been a ball. He loved it and lived it up and wanted me to do the same.

While he was laid out I kept singing at the Uptown House. The second night an old bitch waltzed into the club, heard me, and said, 'You ought to be ashamed of yourself, singing like that while your pop's lying up there in a funeral parlor.'

Until then I had been too broken up to talk to anybody about it. But this bitch was too much for me. I let go and slapped her across the face as hard as I could.

'I know it, I know it,' she answered back. 'You'll never turn out to be anything. You're just cheap.'

This hurt so much I didn't say a damn thing. I just walked away. If I hadn't been sure she was long since dead, I could have sworn this bitch was my cousin Ida. She had her evil sound, her evil ways, and her evil, evil mind.

8

Travelin' Light

Don't tell me about those pioneer chicks hitting the trail in those slip-covered wagons with the hills full of redskins. I'm the girl who went West in 1937 with sixteen white cats, Artie Shaw and his Rolls-Royce – and the hills were full of white crackers.

It all began one night at Clarke Monroe's Uptown House.

Artie came in and got to talking and dreaming about his new band. He thought he needed something sensational to give it a shove.

'Something sensational? That's easy,' I told him. 'Hire a good Negro singer.'

That did it. Artie waited for me all night at the Uptown House and put me right in his car to take me to Boston for the opening. Georgie Auld, Tony Pastor, and Max Kaminsky were with him. Before we left, we drove over to Mom's and she fixed fried chicken for a 6:30 AM breakfast for the whole gang. The chicken knocked Artie out. He never ate anything like she fixed it. When the chicken was gone, we piled into his car and were off.

Boston was jumping then. We were booked in Roseland. Glenn Miller was working just around the corner, and a block away there was Chick Webb and his band with Ella Fitzgerald. Chick's group was the best known; but we were still better known than Miller.

The sight of sixteen men on a bandstand with a Negro girl singer had never been seen before – in Boston or anywhere. The question of how the public would take to it had to be faced opening night at Roseland. Naturally Sy Schribman, the owner of Roseland and a guy who did a lot for bands like Dorsey, Miller, and others, was worried.

But Artie was a guy who never thought in terms of white and colored. 'I can take care of the situation,' was his answer. 'And I know Lady can take care of herself.'

'As far as I'm concerned,' I told Artie, 'I don't care about sitting on the bandstand. When it comes time for me to sing a number, you introduce me, I sing, then I'm gone.'

Artie disagreed. 'No,' he insisted. 'I want you on the bandstand like Helen Forrest and Tony Pastor and everyone else.' So that's what I did. Everything up in Boston was straight – but the real test was coming up. We were heading for Kentucky.

Kentucky is like Baltimore – it's only on the border of being the South, which means the people there take their Dixie stuff more seriously than the crackers farther down.

Right off, we couldn't find a place that would rent me a room. Finally Artie got sore and picked out the biggest hotel in town. He was determined to crack it – or he was going to sue. I tried to stop him. 'Man,' I said, 'are you trying to get me killed?'

Artie had taken the band on the road for a good reason – he wanted to play to as many people as possible before risking a New York opening. The band had enough work to do without looking for lawsuits around every corner and doing a job for the NAACP.

But there was no moving Artie. He's a wild one; he has his own peculiarities but he's amazing and a good cat deep down. He's not one to go back on his word. Whatever he says, Jack, you can believe that's it. Whatever he'd set out to do, he would believe in it. He might find he was wrong, but rather than go back on his word, he'd suffer. That's the way he was and that's why I liked him, and that's why he wouldn't listen to me in Kentucky. He got eight cats out of the band and they escorted me to the registration desk at the biggest hotel in that little old Kentucky town.

I don't think anybody black had ever got a room there before, but the cats in the band acted like it was as natural as breathing. I think the man at the desk figured it couldn't be true what he thought he saw, and I couldn't be a Negro or nobody would act like that. I think they thought I was Spanish or something, so they gave me a nice room and no back talk.

The cats had a little taste of triumph, so they went on from there. All eight of them waltzed into the dining room, carrying me with them like I was the *Queen Mary* and they were a bunch of tug-boats. We sat down, ordered food all around and champagne, acting up like we were a sensation. And we were.

After that scene I guess the management thought they were getting off easy in letting me have a room.

It was a one-man town. And the sheriff was the man. He ran things. He was on the scene that night when we opened in a real-life natural rock cave. The sheriff was haunting the place, letting kids in for half price. They were selling kids whisky right under his nose. But he didn't pay any mind to that. He was too busy dogging me.

When it came time to go on, I told Artie I didn't want any trouble and didn't want to sit on the bandstand.

'It just don't make sense,' I told him. 'This is the damn South.' But Artie didn't want to give in. He was unhappy. I was unhappy. Finally we compromised and agreed I would come out on the stand and sit just before my numbers.

I could smell this sheriff a mile off. I told the cats in the band he was looking for trouble.

'He wants to call me nigger so bad he's going to find a way,' I told them. And so I bet Tony Pastor, Georgie Auld and Max Kaminsky two bucks apiece he would make it.

He did.

When I came on, the sheriff walked up to the raised bandstand; Artie's back was to the dance floor, so he pulled Artie's pants leg and said, 'Hey you!' Artie turned around. 'Don't touch me,' he hollered over the music.

But the sheriff didn't give up so easy. I had money riding on what he would do, so I was watching him real close. So were the cats I had the bet with. They were keeping a free eye on him. He pulled Artie's leg again. 'Hey you,' he said.

Artie turned around. 'You want to get kicked?' he asked him.

Still the old cracker sheriff didn't give up. Back he came again. 'Hey you,' he said. Then he turned to me and, so loud everybody could hear, he said, 'What's Blackie going to sing?'

Artie looked like it was the end of the world – and the tour. I guess he thought I was going to break down and have a collapse or something. But I was laughing like hell. I turned to Georgie, Tony, and Max, put my hand out, and said, 'Come on now, give me the money.'

We had another big scene like this one time in St Louis. We were scheduled to play the ballroom in one of the biggest hotels in town. The man who hired us just leased the ballroom from the hotel. But this day, of all days, after two months of one-nighters and a chance to sit still for three whole weeks, we were rehearsing and in wandered this old cracker who owned the hotel, the city block, the works. He was older than God and hadn't been seen around there in ten years. But he picked this day to come shooting around in his wheel chair to look over his property.

Naturally, the first thing he saw was me. And the first thing he said, was, 'What's that nigger doing there? I don't have niggers to clean up around here.'

Artie tried to tell him I was his vocalist, but he wasn't listening. He wasn't saying anything but 'nigger.'

So I stepped in and said, 'Man, can't you say nothing else? I'm tired of being called nigger.' Besides, I knew I could whip him.

Tony was so sore and red in the face, I didn't know what he might do, when this old cracker ordered Artie and him and me and all of us out of the hotel. If you've got one of those Italian boys like Tony in your corner, they'll go to hell for you and die for you. If one of those cats loves you, I'm sorry, you've got you a buddy-boy.

So with Tony beside me I walked up to this old cracker and stared him down.

'Listen,' I told him. 'Artie Shaw has been very nice to me. I know you don't even have niggers clean up your hotel. But I'm a Negro or whatever you want to call me, and I'll make you a bet. You let us open in this damn ballroom, and if I don't go over better than anyone else, you can throw me and Artie and all of us out. You want to take the bet or don't you?'

He didn't know what to say. He didn't want to take it. But he didn't want to scoot off in his wheel chair either. There were quite a few spectators on the scene, and people began saying he was a drag if he didn't take the bet. So he did, and we opened.

I knew that night I had the future of the whole band riding on me, so I really worked. First I did 'I Cried for You.' Then I followed with 'Them There Eyes.' And then I finished with a thing called 'What You Gonna Do When There Ain't No Swing?' Swing was the thing then.

When I ended the number I held onto the word 'ain't,' then I held 'no.' Then I held my breath, thinking the jury was out and wondering what the verdict would be, and I sang the word 'swing.' I hadn't got the word shaped with my mouth when people stood up whistling and hollering and screaming and clapping. There was no arguing. I was the best, so we stayed there for six weeks instead of three.

It wasn't long before the roughest days with the Basie band began to look like a breeze. I got to the point where I hardly ever ate, slept, or went to the bathroom without having a major NAACP-type production.

Most of the cats in the band were wonderful to me, but I got so tired of scenes in crummy roadside restaurants over getting served, I used to beg Georgie Auld, Tony Pastor, and Chuck Peterson to just let me sit in the bus and rest – and let them bring me out something in a sack. Some places they wouldn't even let me eat in the kitchen. Some places they would. Sometimes it was a choice between me eating and the whole band starving. I got tired of having a federal case over breakfast, lunch, and dinner.

One time we stopped at a dirty little hole in the wall, and the whole band piled in. I was sitting at the counter next to Chuck Peterson. Everybody else gets waited on and this blonde bitch waitress ignores me like I'm not even there. Chuck called her first and then Tony Pastor got real sore. 'This is Lady Day.' He hollered at her, 'Now you feed her.'

I pleaded with him not to start anything, but Tony let loose, the cats in the band started throwing things around. When they wouldn't serve me, the whole band pitched in and wrecked the joint. Everybody grabbed their food, and when the bus pulled out, you could hear the old sheriff's police siren coming after us. Even Artie jumped into that fight.

Getting a night's sleep was a continual drag, too. We were playing big towns and little towns, proms and fairs. A six-hundred-mile jump overnight was standard. When we got to put up at a hotel, it was usually four cats to a room. We might finish at Scranton, Pennsylvania, at two in the morning, grab something to eat, and make Cleveland, Ohio, by noon the next day. The boys in the band had worked out a deal for getting two nights' sleep for one night's rent.

We'd drive all night, hit a town in the morning, register and turn in early, and sleep until time to go to work. When the job was through, we'd sleep the rest of the night, clear out in the morning, and hit the road. This would work every other day and save loot. On the $125 a week I made, that was still very important.

This would have been fine except that I had to double up with another vocalist. I don't think she liked Negroes much, and especially not me. She didn't want to sleep in the same room with me. She only did because she had to.

Artie had asked me to help her to phrase her lyrics; this made her jealous. Then once I made the mistake of telling somebody we got along fine, and to prove it I mentioned how she let me help her phrase. This made her sore. It was true, there were some places where the management wouldn't let me appear, and I'd have to sit in the bus while she did numbers that were arranged for me. She was always happy when she could sing and I couldn't.

I'll never forget the night we were booked at this fancy boys' school in New England. She was real happy because she was sure I was going to have to sit in the bus all night again because I was too black and sexy for those young boys.

But when the time came to open, the head man of the school came out and explained that it wasn't me, they just didn't want any female singers at all. So the two of us had to sit in the bus together all night and listen to the band playing our songs.

Did I razz her! 'You see, honey,' I said, 'you're so fine and grand. You may be white, but you're no better than me. They won't have either of us here because we're both women.'

Almost every day there was an 'incident.'

In a Boston joint they wouldn't let me go in the front door; they wanted me to come in the back way. The cats in the band flipped and said, 'If Lady doesn't go in the front door, the band doesn't go in at all.' So they caved.

Eating was a mess, sleeping was a problem, but the biggest drag of all was a simple little thing like finding a place to go to the bathroom.

Sometimes we'd make a six-hundred-mile jump and only stop once. Then it would be a place where I couldn't get served, let alone crash the toilet without causing a scene. At first I used to be so ashamed. Then finally I just said to hell with it. When I had to go I'd just ask the bus driver to stop and let me off at the side of the road. I'd rather go in the bushes than take a chance in the restaurants and towns.

I kept doing this for so long, come rain and come shine, hot or cold, that it finally began to tell on me. The nervousness and strain finally fixed me so, I was good and sick. Every day riding that bus was torture. I finally went to one old doctor who took one look at me and treated me for clap. He put some packs on me, and that only made it worse.

Finally in Boston one day I couldn't get out of bed and I called my mother. She must have flown up there from New York, she got there so fast. Max Kaminsky played trumpet with us then. He came from Boston and knew his way around. His mother still lived there. She was in her nineties, but when she heard about it she went to bat and sent me a doctor she knew in Boston. He was a woman's specialist. He diagnosed it right – a bad inflammation of the bladder. After I'd gone through three months of torture, this specialist had me on my feet in three days.

When we got to Detroit, we played on the same stage in the same big theater where they tried to black me up because I was too light for the boys in the Basie band. The management never asked me to wear pink make-up to sing with a white band, but if they had I wouldn't have been surprised.

Detroit was almost as far north as we ever went, but it was still full of crackers and I was always uneasy. One night Chuck Peterson asked me to go with him to a little backstage bar on the corner and have a drink. I didn't want to go for the same old reason. But he insisted, and so we did.

In a matter of minutes some woman at the bar piped out that she wasn't going to drink in the place if that nigger stood there, making clear she meant me. Chuck wanted to answer back, but I talked him out of it and we went on to finish our drink.

The next thing we knew, a man came over and started after Chuck. 'What the hell's going on?' he said. 'A man can't bring his wife in a bar any more without you tramp white men bringing a nigger woman in.'

Chuck wouldn't stand for that, but before he knew it this guy and a couple more were on him, beating and kicking him. While everyone else stood around with their mouths open, this guy kept kicking Chuck in the mouth and saying, 'I'll fix it so you don't play trumpet tonight.'

If my maid hadn't come in just then from backstage to tell me it was show time and helped me get him out of there, they might have beat him to death.

I was sick for the rest of the booking in Detroit. Eventually Chuck's mother, who happens to be a lawyer, sued the management for damages and collected a few thousand dollars.

There's something weird about that town. Ten years later, it didn't seem so much better. When I was headlining at the Paradise Theater in Detroit's Negro section in 1949, I walked in a nearby bar. The bartender greeted me by telling me he couldn't serve me because I had enough.

I asked him what he meant. 'Do you really think I had enough or don't you serve Negroes?'

'There she goes,' he said, 'trying to start trouble. She must be drunk.'

The next time there was a riot in Detroit, I heard that this particular little saloon got taken apart.

There are traces of most of my musical days around on records. But the period with Artie is a big gap. That's because the two of us got in a squeeze between two record labels. I was under contract to Columbia. They issued my records on their thirty-five-cent Vocalion label. Artie was under contract to Victor. When we wanted to do some sides together, Columbia agreed it would be O.K. for me to record with Artie and his band because Victor would release them and sell them for seventy-five cents a side. That wasn't considered competition.

So we did a few things together. But when the time came to release them, Victor decided to issue them on their thirty-five-cent label, Bluebird records. Columbia naturally flipped at this. Why should anyone pay thirty-five cents to hear Billie Holiday when they could get Holiday and Artie Shaw and his whole damn band for the same price? I was in the middle. So was Artie.

But Columbia made Victor call them all in – all they could. A few got out, though. Everybody was sore.

After we'd been out for a few months, we were back in New York one day and I was living at the Plymouth Hotel and Artie came by and asked me to come down in the street for a big surprise. He collected everybody he could find to come down in front of the hotel and see the big old Rolls-Royce he'd bought for himself.

Now a Rolls-Royce may be the greatest thing on wheels, but standing there at the curb, it was a funny-looking son of a gun.

From then on Artie used to lead the caravan driving this big old Rolls. And he always wanted me to ride up with him and Max and Tony and sometimes Benny, our road manager. I had mixed feelings about this. A Rolls is built for pleasure. It's great to be able to call your chauffeur and say, 'James, take me through Central Park and back home.' It's fine to pull up in front of El Morocco or somewhere and have it wait to take your black ass home. But it's nowhere for highballing a hundred and fifty miles to make a gig. You take it up over thirty-five miles an hour and if you're in the back seat it's apt to turn you into a milkshake.

You got to sit up straight in it like a queen cruising past her subjects. It's no damn good for lovers either. You can't bend in it no kind of way. It's only good for one thing – that's to be dicty.

So I used to ride up with Artie in the Rolls and get shaken around like crazy while Artie tired himself out to get his kicks out of driving. And because the other vocalist would have to ride in the bus, she thought she was suffering from discrimination, and that would make her even saltier with me.

One of the reasons Artie had me ride with him was that often he would talk to me when he was talking to nobody else – not even Willard Alexander, the big wheel booking the band.

Sometimes I'd walk in his hotel suite and take one look at him and know that that day he was Mister Shaw and he didn't want to be messed with. Other days he was 'Old Man,' or 'Artie,' or 'Hey, man.' Sometimes he would want to get lost on his farm without shaving for months, staying in this one pair of overalls, the way he did when he retired and wrote 'Back Bay Shuffle.'

But I knew his moods and I respected them and he knew it. I figured they were his business. He was like me, he never hurt anyone but himself.

But after surviving months of being bugged by sheriffs, waitresses, hotel clerks, and crackers of kinds in the South, I got the crummiest deal of all when we got back to New York – New York, my own home town.

We were set to open at the Blue Room of Maria Kramer's Lincoln on 43rd Street. The Lincoln hadn't been a good spot for bands, but there was a coast-to-coast radio wire in the room – and in those days radio was everything. This was my chance to sing on the radio coast to coast every night. A few weeks of this and any band or any singer could be made. This was big time.

I should have known something was shaking when the hotel management gave me a suite. I didn't need a place to sleep. I was staying home with Mom. I didn't even need a place to dress. I could come to the hotel every night dressed, and Artie always wanted me to sit on the bandstand all night and look pretty, anyway.

Artie was getting pressure from all over – the hotel, the booking agency, the networks. But he didn't have the heart to tell me. The excuse for giving me the suite was that I was supposed to stay there until it was time for me to sing, and not mingle with the guests.

The next thing I knew, the management wanted me to come in

the back door of the hotel. When a little joint in Boston tried this, the whole band had said, 'If Lady doesn't use the front door, the band doesn't either.' But Artie and the cats in the band had taken months of hell for this New York engagement, and nobody was in a position to push a hotel chain, a broadcasting network, and the talent agency around.

So I had to come in the back door. I don't know why I didn't walk out then and there, except Mom got such a kick out of listening to our nightly broadcasts. She was crazy about sitting home and hearing me on the radio.

The next thing I knew, I was singing less and less. Some nights I'd only be on for one song all night – and that would be before or after the band had been on the air.

Finally, when they cut me off the air completely, I said to hell with it. I just fired myself. I told Artie he should have told me when the big wheels cracked down on him. 'Down South I can dig this kind of stuff, but I can't take it in New York.'

The sheriff in Kentucky was at least honest. A real good cracker says, 'I don't like Negroes period.' Or 'dot,' as they say in the South. Some just say, 'I don't want to socialize with Negroes.' They don't tell you that behind your back, they tell it right to your face, and you know it. A cracker just wants you to clean up his house or take care of his kids and then get the hell out.

Even when they insult you they do it to your face. That's the only way they can let you know they're superior to you. They might die and leave you all their money, but somewhere in the fine print in that will they've got to let you know you were a good nigger but you're still a nigger.

This sheriff in Kentucky called me 'Blackie' to my face. The big-deal hotels, agencies, and networks in New York were giving me a fast shove behind my back.

I had been with Artie a year and a half. We had had some real times. I'll always remember the night I sat on the piano bench in his hotel suite, looking across the Boston Back Bay for twelve hours, pounding out two bass notes while he finished writing his theme song, 'Nightmare.'

There aren't many people who fought harder than Artie against the vicious people in the music business or the crummy side of second-class citizenship which eats at the guts of so many musicians. He didn't win. But he didn't lose either. It wasn't long after I left that he told them to shove it like I had. And people still talk about him as if he were nuts because there were things more important to him than a million damn bucks a year.

9

Sunny Side of the Street

It's only five miles – thirty-five minutes by the IRT – from Pod's and Jerry's at 133rd Street off Seventh Avenue to Sheridan Square, near Fourth Street on the same avenue. But the places were worlds apart and it took about seven years to make the trip.

The next big thing that happened to me was at Café Society Downtown. It was just a basement full of people mopping, cleaning, dusting, painting murals, and a hopeful notion of a Jersey shoe manufacturer named Barney Josephson when I first went down there. I met him through John Hammond.

Barney and his wife, a really wonderful girl, told me this was to be one club where there was going to be no segregation, no racial prejudice. 'Everybody's going to be for real in here.'

This was what I'd been waiting for. I was so happy. The opening bill included Meade Lux Lewis, the two-piano boogie-woogie team of Albert Ammons and Pete Johnson, Joe Turner, and Frank Newton had the band.

I'll never forget that opening night. There must have been six hundred people in the joint, celebrities, artists, rich society people. And a big hitch. Barney had his liquor license, but nobody could go on until we had the cabaret license – and it hadn't arrived. It got to be eleven o'clock, and we were getting panicky. The cops were standing by.

I couldn't stand the suspense any longer. 'Come on, let's take a chance,' I told Barney. 'One night in jail isn't going to hurt anybody.'

We had already decided to take the chance and go on at eleven-thirty, when the license arrived at the last minute, like the Marines. So with the cops standing by, we went on. Meade Lux Lewis knocked them out; Ammons and Johnson flipped them; Joe Turner killed them; Newton's band sent them; and then I came on. This was an audience.

It was during my stint at Café Society that a song was born which became my personal protest – 'Strange Fruit.' The germ of the song was in a poem written by Lewis Allen. I first met him at Café Society. When he showed me that poem, I dug it right off. It seemed to spell out all the things that had killed Pop.

Allen, too, had heard how Pop died and of course was interested in my singing. He suggested that Sonny White, who had been my accompanist, and I turn it into music. So the three of us got together and did the job in about three weeks. I also got a wonderful assist from Danny Mendelsohn, another writer who had done arrangements for me. He helped me with arranging the song and rehearsing it patiently. I worked like the devil on it because I was never sure I could put it across or that I could get across to a plush night-club audience the things that it meant to me.

I was scared people would hate it. The first time I sang it I thought it was a mistake and I had been right being scared. There wasn't even a patter of applause when I finished. Then a lone person began to clap nervously. Then suddenly everyone was clapping.

It caught on after a while and people began to ask for it. The version I recorded for Commodore became my biggest-selling record. It still depresses me every time I sing it, though. It reminds me of how Pop died. But I have to keep singing it, not only because people ask for it but because twenty years after Pop died the things that killed him are still happening in the South.

Over the years I've had a lot of weird experiences as a result of that song. It has a way of separating the straight people from the squares and cripples. One night in Los Angeles a bitch stood right up in the club where I was singing and said, 'Billie, why don't you sing that sexy song you're so famous for? You know, the one about the naked bodies swinging in the trees.'

Needless to say, I didn't.

But another time, on 52nd Street, I finished a set with 'Strange

Fruit' and headed, as usual, for the bathroom. I always do. When I sing it, it affects me so much I get sick. It takes all the strength out of me.

This woman came in the ladies' room at the Downbeat Club and found me all broken up from crying. I had come off the floor running, hot and cold, miserable and happy. She looked at me, and the tears started coming to her eyes. 'My God,' she said, 'I never heard anything so beautiful in my life. You can still hear a pin drop out there.'

Just a few months ago in a club in Miami I had run through an entire two-week date without ever doing 'Strange Fruit.' I was in no mood to be bothered with the scenes that always come on when I do that number in the South. I didn't want to start anything I couldn't finish. But one night after everybody had asked me twenty times to do it, I finally gave in. There was a special character who had haunted the club for days, always asking for 'Strange Fruit' and 'Gloomy Sunday.' I don't know why he wanted to hear either one. He looked like Gloomy Sunday to me. But I finally gave them what they asked for as an encore.

When I came to the final phrase of the lyrics I was in the angriest and strongest voice I had been in for months. My piano player was in the same kind of form. When I said, '. . . for the sun to rot,' and then a piano punctuation, '. . . for the wind to suck,' I pounced on those words like they had never been hit before.

I was flailing the audience, but the applause was like nothing I'd ever heard. I came off, went upstairs, changed into street clothes, and when I came down they were still applauding.

Not many other singers ever tried to do 'Strange Fruit.' I never tried to discourage them, but audiences did. Years after me at Café Society, Josh White came on with his guitar and his shirt front split down to here and did it. The audience shouted for him to leave the song alone.

A few years later Lillian Smith told me the song inspired her to write the novel and the play about a lynching. You know what she called it.

*

During my two years at Café Society I got taken up by some of the people the joint was named after. They tried, anyway. I met a lot of nice people. But I met a lot of drags too. I became a celebrity, and when that happens, watch out.

When I was thirteen I got real evil one time and set in my ways. I just plain decided one day I wasn't going to do anything or say anything unless I meant it. Not 'Please, sir.' Not 'Thank you, ma'am.' Nothing. Unless I meant it.

You have to be poor and black to know how many times you can get knocked in the head just for trying to do something as simple as that.

But I never gave up trying. And I tried to do it whether it was on my own home ground in Harlem or on somebody else's.

I found out the main difference between uptown and down-town was people are more for real up there. They got to be, I guess. Uptown a whore was a whore; a pimp was a pimp; a thief was a thief; a faggot was a faggot; a dike was a dike; a mother-hugger was a mother-hugger.

Downtown it was different – more complicated. A whore was sometimes a socialite; a pimp could be a man about town; a thief could be an executive; a faggot could be a playboy; a dike might be called a deb; a mother-hugger was somebody who wasn't adjusted and had problems.

I always had trouble keeping this double talk straight. And sometimes when I messed up, the fur and feathers would fly so you'd think nobody around there ever called a spade a spade before.

'What will people think?' is a big deal in ofay circles. It never mattered a damn to me, but I got interested in the way it worked and saw what it did to people who cared.

There was a girl, for instance, I first met at Café Society and got to know pretty well. I'm going to call her Brenda. She was a good-looking chick about my age. She lived on Fifth Avenue in a big apartment full of money. Her family had a corner of the paper busi-ness or something. Every time she blew her nose she made some more loot.

She came around night after night. She was crazy about my

singing and used to wait for me to finish up. I wasn't blind. I hadn't been on Welfare Island for nothing. It wasn't long before I knew I had become a thing for this girl. It got embarrassing. But I felt sorry for her too. Before long she got to depend on seeing me and being around. And I working in a public place. I couldn't tell her I was sick and then show up for three shows a night. I couldn't very well use the doorman for a maid and have him tell her I wasn't home.

Then she started buying and sending me presents – slacks and jackets, suits cut and tailored like a man's with butchy accessories.

This made no kind of sense. I might not be a lot of things, but one look at me and you can mark me down as a girl-type girl. No charge account at Abercrombie & Fitch could change that.

But there we were, a rich white heiress from Fifth Avenue and a Negro girl from uptown. Yet I could hang around on Fifth Avenue with Brenda and nobody so much as batted an eye – not the uniformed doorman, neighbors, servants, nobody, not even her mother. For all anybody cared, we could have been a couple of college girls out on a field trip studying race relations or some other damn kind of conditions.

But just let me walk out of the club one night with a young white boy of my age, whether it was John Roosevelt, the President's son, or Joe Blow. Let us go around the corner to get a drink, and every sonofabitch and his brother would have his tongue out and be prepared to go to court and swear we were having a hot old affair and what will people think?

They still make it hot for a Negro girl who walks to the corner with a white man. But a black chick and a white chick can be married and carrying on and everything's cool as far as the what-will-people-think people are concerned.

This is a mess for Negroes and a mess for white people. I've known black chicks in show business who were as feminine as me, but before long they got acting like lezzies because it's so easy, and all the pressure is that way, and it's less trouble.

But some girls like Brenda are sadder still. They can't love or let themselves go with anybody – man or woman. They can't even be lesbians and work at it. They're incapable of loving anybody – just the opposite of my trouble. And they try to make up for it by buying things for people like me.

It's a cinch to see how it all begins. These poor bitches grow up hating their mothers and having the hots for their fathers. And since being in love with our father is taboo, they grow up unable to get any kicks out of anything unless it's taboo too. And since Negroes in America walk around with big 'Do Not Touch' signs on them, that's where we come in. And I'm telling you it can be a drag.

Sometimes simple little mess-ups like this take years to unravel; and that's how these doctors with the couches make their loot.

Brenda was always trying to do something for me – and when she ran out of ideas for things she could do for me she would try my mother.

Mom had always dreamed of having a real honest-to-God restaurant of her own with a framed license on the wall from the Board of Health. She wanted to give up that combination fried-chicken parlor and after-hours soup kitchen for Local 802 and go legit. Mom was always after me to invest some loot in this project. But I never could see it and never seemed to have enough loot. She had saved a few hundred of the bucks I had cleaned out of the Basie band shooting crap on the bus, but that wasn't enough.

One night Mom was campaigning for her damn restaurant when Brenda was at the house. Right off she offered to be an angel for the project.

It was her way of keeping tight with me, but it was what Mom wanted. So she started planning and eventually ended up with a place of her own, Mom Holiday's, on 99th Street near Columbus.

I didn't fight it because it kept Mom busy and happy and stopped her from worrying and watching over me.

It wasn't long before I was sorry. Going legit couldn't change the Duchess. Nobody could just be a customer. They were all people and she loved them. Half of Local 802 was soon hanging around. All you had to do was say you were a musician or a friend of mine and you could get anything in the joint.

Cats could come in, order themselves a big feed, then give her a story instead of money. Then sometimes Mom would give them some change on the way out. She was always giving change for money she never saw.

The best paying customer she had was me. Every time I went in the place I paid for something.

One time she'd have a long face on, waiting for me.

'The Board of Health was here,' she'd say. 'They said we got to have two toilets.'

The damn Board of Health could pass by thousands of Harlem tenements with no damn toilets at all, then land on the Duchess and tell her she had to have two.

So it would take a few hundred bucks for that. Then the next time I'd turn around she'd say, 'The Board of Health was here again. They say I can't fry hamburgers in a pan any more. I got to have a griddle.'

So I handed over another few bucks for a griddle. Fifty for this. And forty for that. I don't know how much it cost me to keep the Board of Health happy, but it was plenty. And I never got back a quarter.

I only tried once. And neither me nor Mom ever forgot it. I needed some money one night and I knew Mom was sure to have some. So I walked in the restaurant like a stockholder and asked.

Mom turned me down flat. She wouldn't give me a cent. She was mad with me and I was mad with her. We exchanged a few words. Then I said, 'God bless the child that's got his own,' and walked out.

I stayed sore for three weeks. I thought about it and thought about it. One day a whole damn song fell into place in my head. Then I rushed down to the Village that night and met Arthur Herzog. He sat down at a piano and picked it out, phrase by phrase, as I sang to him.

I couldn't wait to get it down and get it recorded. I told him about the fight with Mom and how I wanted to get even. We changed the lyrics in a couple of spots, but not much.

This one will gas the Duchess, I thought. And it did.

GOD BLESS THE CHILD*

Them that's got shall get
Them that's not shall lose
So the Bible says
And it still is news
Mama may have
Papa may have
But God bless the child that's got his own
That's got his own.
Yes, the strong gets more
While the weak ones fade
Empty pockets don't
Ever make the grade
Mama may have
Papa may have
But God bless the child that's got his own
That's got his own.

Money, you've got lots of friends
Crowding round your door
But when it's done
And spending ends
They don't come no more
Rich relations give
Crust of bread and such
You can help yourself but don't take much
Mama may have
Papa may have
But God bless the child that's got his own
That's got his own.

I stayed at Café Society steady for two years, seven nights a week, no nights off, for seventy-five dollars a week.

* Copyright, 1941, by E. R. Marks.

One night a little girl came in with her mother and wanted to audition. Barney had turned her down when I heard about it. We had quite a little row in my dressing room over it. I told him to give the girl a chance, what did he have to lose? Barney refused, said she wasn't pretty – she was too dark.

'Too dark?' I asked him. 'Hell, this is supposed to be a cosmopolitan joint. What do you care what she looks like as long as she's got talent?'

'Besides,' I told him, 'I need a vacation and I'm going to take one.'

So Barney gave an audition to this dark little girl in her pink mammy-made dress. She played the piano real good. I got my vacation, and Miss Hazel Scott got the job.

The Moon Looks Down and Laughs

I opened Café Society as an unknown; I left two years later as a star. But you couldn't tell the difference from what I had in my sock. I was still making that same old seventy-five dollars a week. I had made more than that in Harlem. I needed the prestige and publicity all right, but you can't pay rent with it. Joe Glaser was supposed to be my manager and getting me more loot, but it didn't work out that way.

So when I left I got tough with my manager and demanded $250 a week in theaters and $175 a week in clubs. The first job I got at $175 a week was one I got myself in a new joint in the San Fernando Valley. And I made my first trip to California.

The valley joint belonged to Red Colonna, Jerry's brother. Jerry had put up the dough and they decided to call it Café Society. They had no business using the name. Barney had copyrighted it, and in the legal scuffle over that we got closed up after the third week. But Red was a wild one and I had my kicks while it lasted.

Martha Raye was married to David Rose then, and they used to come in the joint every night and fight. She loved him, but they couldn't make it. Martha loves to ball. She's my girl, I'm crazy about her.

A lot of the real dicty people with talent used to come and hear me. They were wonderful to sing to, but as usual it only took one cracker in the audience to wreck things. I had just started doing 'Strange Fruit' then; the record was selling and I always got a request for it in about every show.

I remember the night this white boy stayed around just to bug me. When I started singing it, he'd start kicking up a storm of noise, rattling glasses, calling me nigger, and cursing nigger singers.

After two shows of this I was ready to quit. I knew if I didn't the third time round I might bounce something off that cracker and land in some San Fernando ranch-type jail. I didn't have fifteen cents on me, and if I walked out I didn't know how I was going to get out of the valley, but I was quitting anyway.

It was then that Bob Hope came in. He came over to me, God bless him, with Jerry Colonna and Judy Garland and I'll never forget it.

'Listen,' said Hope, 'you go out there and sing. Let that sonofabitch say something and I'll take care of him.'

So I did, and he did. It was a real mess. When the cracker boy started, I stopped singing and Bob took the floor. Hope traded insults with that cracker for five minutes before he had enough and left. After Hope had finished him, I went back singing.

When I did my last encore, the joint was still ringing with applause and Bob Hope was waiting for me in the dining room with a big bucket of champagne. I hate champagne, but I drank it that night. After a couple of swigs I looked around and the mirrors in the joint were shaking and the chandeliers were swinging.

'Man, this is powerful stuff,' I said. I took the glass and raised it as a toast to Hope. I thought he looked a little pale. 'Look, Bob,' I said. 'I don't usually drink the stuff, but this champagne is crazy.'

'Look, girl,' he said, 'don't you know we just now had one of the worst earthquakes anybody ever had around here?'

It was another big night at the joint in the valley the night I met Orson Welles. Orson was in Hollywood for the first time, like me. I liked him and he liked me, and jazz. We started hanging around together.

So when I'd finished at the joint in the valley, we'd head for Central Avenue, the Negro ghetto of Los Angeles, and I'd take him around all the joints and dives. I was bored with all this stuff; I'd grown up in it, there was nothing anybody in California could show me, anything there was doing out there, I'd seen before and sideways. I was bored, but he loved it.

There wasn't a damn thing or person he wasn't interested in. He wanted to see everything and find out who and why it ticked. I guess that's part of what made him such a great artist.

Orson was up to his ears then making his first picture, *Citizen Kane*, was writing, directing, and acting all over the place. He might be out balling, but his head seemed to be going all the time, thinking about what was going to happen at the studio the next morning at 6 AM. *Citizen Kane* was a great picture. I'll bet I saw it nine times before it played in any theaters. He was such a hell of an actor, I never missed the scenery or the costumes.

After we'd been seen together a few times I started getting phone calls at my hotel telling me I was ruining Orson's career by being seen with him. People used to bug me, saying the studio would get after me, that I'd never get to work in pictures, and God knows what, if I didn't leave him alone. The hotel used to get the same kind of calls from people trying to make trouble for me or for him.

A lot of creeps have been dogging Orson Welles ever since but they can't touch him. He's a fine cat – probably the finest I ever met. And a talented cat. But more than that, he's fine people.

It isn't much better now, but back then people used to flip at seeing a white man with a Negro girl. It could be Marian Anderson with her agent; or a shake dancer with her pimp. It doesn't matter how unlikely the couple, the mother-hugging squares always figure they're only up to one damn thing. Maybe they were, maybe they weren't. If they weren't, they might just as well have been, because no damn body would believe they had any damn reason for being together unless they just got out of bed or were headed there.

This makes life a continual drag. Not only for me, but for people I meet and like. You're always under pressure. You can fight it but you can't lick it.

The only time I was free from this kind of pressure was when I was a call girl as a kid and I had white men as my customers. Nobody gave us any trouble. People can forgive people any damn thing if they did it for money.

One day in Hollywood I went out for a drive with this rich young blonde starlet. She was running around with Billy Daniels, whom I used to work with back at the Hotcha. Billy had loaned her his pretty Cadillac to drive around in. She was taking me to the aquarium, when boom, this brand-new fishtail stopped and we couldn't start it.

There we sat out on this deserted spot near the beach. I knew from nothing about a car and she knew damn little more. I thought we were stranded until I saw a car down the road a piece. There was a cat lying under it, tinkering around, and he looked like he knew what he was doing.

So I hailed him. 'Hey, man,' I said, 'there's a couple of chicks in distress over here. How about coming over and seeing what's wrong?' When he crawled out from under the car he had sunglasses on, but he looked familiar. I said, 'I know you from some damn where.' He was real nice; he recognized me from having been over to the joint in the valley and heard me sing.

It only took him about two minutes to find out what was wrong and to fix it. Then he got behind the wheel and drove the car for a little to make sure everything was all right before he left us. Then he asked us if we wouldn't like to stop and have a drink. I was ready, so he drove us up to a big fancy country club or something right near the beach.

We walked in the bar and people were all eyes. I didn't think anything of it. That was always happening. But there has to be one joker everywhere. And there was one there at the bar. When he finally got loaded enough he walked over to our table; he stared me up and down. Then he stared the blonde up and down. Then he turned to our mechanic friend and said, 'Well, I see you get all the dames.'

It wasn't until our mechanic buddy got up from behind the table and flattened this cracker to the floor that I came to. It was Clark Gable who'd given us the lift.

He laughed when I told him I recognized him by his fist work.

When I came home from Hollywood I was dressed a little sharper than when I went out. I'd learned a few tricks about make-up from those Hollywood bitches, but otherwise I came home to Mom the same old way, on a bus and poor as the day I was born.

II

I Can't Get Started

You can be up to your boobies in white satin, with gardenias in your hair and no sugar cane for miles, but you can still be working on a plantation.

Take 52nd Street in the late thirties and early forties. It was supposed to be a big deal. 'Swing Street,' they called it. Joint after joint was jumping. It was this 'new' kind of music. They could get away with calling it new because millions of squares hadn't taken a trip to 131st Street. If they had they could have dug swing for twenty years.

By the time the ofays got around to copping 'swing' a new-style music was already breaking out all over uptown. Ten years later that became the newest thing when the white boys downtown figured out how to cop it.

Anyway, white musicians were 'swinging' from one end of 52nd Street to the other, but there wasn't a black face in sight on the street except Teddy Wilson and me. Teddy played intermission piano at the Famous Door and I sang. There was no cotton to be picked between Leon and Eddie's and the East River, but man, it was a plantation any way you looked at it. And we had to not only look at it, we lived in it. We were not allowed to mingle any kind of way. The minute we were finished with our intermission stint we had to scoot out back to the alley or go out and sit in the street.

Teddy had an old beat-up Ford he used to drive to work in. Sometimes we'd just go out and sit in it parked at the curb.

There was a wild cat who used to come around the joint all the time and he drove a crazy foreign car. Every time he got in it to take off, it sounded like a B-29, and the Famous Door management didn't like that. Anyway, we got friendly with him, and he got friendly with us, and it cost both Teddy and me our first jobs on 52nd Street. We got our asses fraternized right off the street.

He was a young millionaire living it up and nobody was going to tell him what to do, who to drink with and who not to drink with. He'd come in the joint and listen to me and Teddy and always wanted to buy us drinks. He insisted we ball with him. And as much as they wanted to please a big spender, both the boss and the headwaiter insisted we didn't.

We told him we were under orders not to socialize with the customers, but he'd insist back that nobody was going to give him orders. Finally one night after he'd bugged me so and practically made me feel like a Tom for not sitting down with him, I got fed up and did.

We had a couple drinks together, and they were my last ones in that joint for a while. When I got up, the boss told me to go pick up my papers, I was fired. He was nasty enough to fire Teddy, too, although Teddy hadn't done a thing. After this big scandal which might ruin him on the street, he said he didn't want any Negroes in the place at all.

I burned. I had to get out, but I hated like hell to go home and tell Mom I'd been bounced again – over something as silly as this. So our millionaire friend tried to cheer us up. We went off with him in his fancy foreign car and drove uptown through Central Park in that crazy-assed wagon in three minutes.

He told us not to worry, he had plenty of money and there were plenty of jobs. And besides, he was a musician and going to have his own damn dance band soon and everything would be fine.

'Yeah,' I told him, 'big deal. You've got plenty of money, but in the meantime you've ruined my life so I don't even dare go home. What's going to happen to Teddy and me?'

So he said, 'Don't go home, let's ball a little.' We wound up back at the Uptown House. Everyone insisted I get up and sing. So I did. And they offered me a regular job again back at the old stand.

Our millionaire friend kept his word, too. He pulled a few wires and got Teddy a job in a radio studio band. He also kept his word and ended up with his own band – and a good one. He was Charlie Barnet.

★

But 52nd Street couldn't hold the line against Negroes forever. Something had to give. And eventually it was the plantation owners. They found they could make money off Negro artists and they couldn't afford their old prejudices. So the barriers went down, and it gave jobs to a lot of great musicians.

I went into Ralph Watkins' Kelly's Stables as a headliner, no more intermission stuff. The typical bill I appeared with in those days would cost plenty today. One time there was Coleman Hawkins' band, me and Stuff Smith, and for intermission Nat Cole and his trio. Nobody in the joint got two hundred a week. I was there for two years at a top of $175 and I was the star. Then there was Roy Eldridge's band, Una Mae Carlisle, Lips Page and his group, and the great Art Tatum playing intermission piano.

Working on the street seemed like a homecoming every night. People I'd met in Harlem, Hollywood, and Café Society used to come in and there was always some kind of reunion. I was getting a little billing and publicity, so my old friends and acquaintances knew where to find me.

On my first trip to the West Coast the valley joint had folded up under me and we had an earthquake to boot. My second trip a couple of years later was a little better – but as soon as I got on the scene we had another earthquake. Everybody finds unusual weather out there.

At least on my second trip West I wasn't alone. Lester had left the Basie Organization by then and he went out with me to work at Billy Berg's.

This was a different kind of place – not high class enough to be high class and not low class enough to be a dive. It was out near the valley – but not too far out like Red Colonna's had been. That first place couldn't live without movie people. Some nights you'd get Gable, another night Garland. But they came one at a time, and it took 150 people to keep that joint from rattling. And the trouble with movie people is they've got everything at home. It takes something different or great to drag them out, especially when they got those 6 AM dates with the make-up man in the morning. And Hollywood was booming in those days.

It was a crazy group Lester assembled at Billy's place. I can hear them now even though I can't remember all their proper names. We had a little trumpet player who sounded like Buck Clayton, only he sang more; and Bumps Mayers, a California man; two tenors and a trumpet. Lester had his brother Lee on drums and a nice ofay cat on piano and Red Kallen on bass.

We used to rock that joint. Bette Davis came in one night and danced herself crazy. Lana Turner used to come in every Tuesday and Thursday. That girl can really dance, and she did at Billy's. She always asked me for 'Strange Fruit' and 'Gloomy Sunday.' She used to like to dance with young Mel Tormé, who used to win all of Billy's lindy contests. Maybe he couldn't cut the cats at the Savoy in Harlem, but he sure could dance.

He was like me when I was a kid, in a way, wanting to make it as a dancer and not interested in singing. And he was a switch on me in another way. My singing voice is clear but my speaking voice is husky; Mel's speaking voice was clear but his singing voice sounded sort of cloudy and foggy. I tried to tell him he had something different in the way of sound and encouraged him to try singing. He never seemed to want to listen. Maybe a lot of other people told him the same thing, but anyway, I was pleased later to hear he was making it. I always liked his singing, too. No matter what he was doing, he wasn't imitating anybody and he had that beat.

Another raggedy youngster I met at Billy's in those days is a big man today. He was as broke as me and Lester then. We used to sit on a fence out back of the joint, talking big and dreaming big, and then pool our money to go off and buy Chinese food. He had a good mind and loved jazz. 'John Hammond thinks he's something,' he used to say. 'Someday I'm going to be really big, and when I do I'm going to do something for Negro jazz musicians.' He got there and he did, and he's been a good friend of mine from that day to this, Norman Granz.

This was the time when Billy Eckstine's band was playing at the Plantation Club in Los Angeles. Lester and I used to sneak over there and catch Billy's group and the new things they were doing. Sarah Vaughan was singing with Billy then and just getting started.

It brought back the rough old days with the Basie band to see the way those kids had to work.

All of them, including Sarah, wore some damn uniforms and they were a mess. I used to try to get Billy to get Sarah a couple of gowns, but he wouldn't get her a spool of thread. He had his troubles, I guess, making payroll at the end of the week. But I looked at it from Sarah's viewpoint. If I had to work like she worked, I'd have died of shame.

Even in the worst Basie days I paid the cleaners for cleaning and pressing my gowns before I ate. And I knew what a hassle it was to keep your foot out of your mouth on the road on the salary that chick was making. So when Billy couldn't do nothing to help, I went to see a dame I knew who sold me a beautiful three-hundred-dollar evening gown for a song. I went out to the Plantation and gave it to Sarah. She didn't know where the gown came from and I didn't tell her. But the moment she put it on she looked more like a girl who was going somewhere. And she did, and I was happy she did.

During my first Hollywood earthquake I was drinking champagne with Bob Hope. My second one happened while I was balling at Joe Louis' place. There was a mob of people there, but I was leaving early because I had a recording date the next day and I had a helluva toothache.

There was a young cat there who told me he had something for my toothache and asked me to come outside. When we got out, it turned out he had some pot. He gave me some of it, told me to put it in my tooth, and we stood there underneath this big tree and smoked up the rest. I was in the middle of a drag on this cigarette when the damnedest feeling came over me. It came so fast and was over so fast, I didn't know what had happened. But this young cat was smart; he gave me a shove that landed me on the ground a few feet away, and there was a whoom and this big tree crashed over with a wham and a bang.

It just wasn't my time, I guess. Joe had driven off just a few seconds before then in his car with some girl and they didn't feel a thing.

It only lasted two or three seconds, but when we went back in

Joe's house every damn glass and dish in the place was broken. Furniture was upside down and people were running around screaming. One of Joe's friends had been upstairs with some broad, sneaking himself a little time, and he came running down the stairs half dressed, and half out of his head screaming, 'Joe, save me!'

I stopped this son of a gun and told him to go back up and finish dressing. 'Joe needs somebody to save *him* and he ain't even here.'

12

Mother's Son-in-Law

I'm not the first – or last – chick who got married to try to prove something to somebody. From the time I started hanging out with Jimmy Monroe, both Mom and Joe Glaser never stopped telling me I was going to get hurt. They said he'd never marry me. That got my spite up. Nobody was going to tell me that.

Jimmy was the younger brother of Clarke Monroe, who ran the Uptown House. He was the most beautiful man I'd laid eyes on since Buck Clayton. He had been married to Nina Mae McKinney, who was a big dancing and singing star. I had seen her in movies like *Hallelujah* when I was a kid. Jimmy had been in Europe for quite a while. Over there, especially in England, as the big beautiful husband of a big star, he had been quite a big deal himself.

In London he had hung out with nothing but white women. He had brought at least one big beautiful Cockney chick back to New York with him. He was managing her when I met him.

He had picked her up in London, made a lady out of her, taught her how to sing, how to talk and act fancy. He came back from England tourist class, but he brought her along first class.

He was a big deal, I figured, what would he want with me?

When this British dame heard Jimmy was going around with me, she even called my mother and tried to scare her into heckling me into staying away from him. That was where Mom got that news that he would never marry me.

Things had happened to me that no amount of time could change or heal. I had gone to jail when I was ten because a forty-year-old man had tried to rape me. Sure they had no more business putting me in that Catholic institution than if I'd been hit by a damn truck.

But they did. Sure, they had no business punishing me, but they had. For years I used to dream about it and wake up hollering and screaming. My God, it's terrible what something like this does to you. It takes years and years to get over it; it haunts you and haunts you.

Getting booked and busted again didn't help, either. I might explain the first rap was a freak accident. But the second was tougher. For years it made me feel like a damn cripple. It changed the way I looked at everything and everybody. There was one chance I couldn't take. I couldn't stand any man who didn't know about the things that had happened to me when I was a kid. And I was leery of any man who could throw those things back at me in a quarrel. I could take almost anything, but my God, not that. I didn't want anyone around who might ever hold this over me or even hint that on account of it he was a cut above me.

Maybe that's part of why I was attracted to Jimmy. He had been around. He had a little past of his own. He was what he was, but in that field he was tops. Besides, he had taste and class.

The taste, the class, and the gloss were what Mom saw. It was all Joe Glaser saw. That's why they warned me to take it easy, that he would never marry me. This meant only one thing to me. That they thought Jimmy might think he was too good for me. That did it.

The first thing I did after Jimmy and I eloped to Elkton, Maryland, in September of 1941, was to go home to Mom and throw the marriage license at her. Then I went up to Joe Glaser's office and threw it at him. I showed them, and that's for damn sure.

One of the songs I wrote and recorded has my marriage to Jimmy Monroe written all over it. I guess I always knew what I was letting myself in for when he married me. I knew this beautiful white English girl was still in town. He didn't admit it, of course. But I knew. One night he came in with lipstick on his collar. Mom had moved to the Bronx by then, and we were staying there when we were in New York.

I saw the lipstick. He saw I saw it and he started explaining and explaining. I could stand anything but that. Lying to me was worse than anything he could have done with any bitch. I cut him off, just like that. 'Take a bath, man,' I said, 'don't explain.'

That should have been the end of it. But that night stuck in my crop. I couldn't forget it. The words 'don't explain, don't explain' kept going through my damn head. I had to get it out of my system some way, I guess. The more I thought about it, it changed from an ugly scene to a sad song. Soon I was singing phrases to myself. Suddenly I had a whole song.

I went downtown one night and sat down with Arthur Herzog; he played the tune over on the piano, wrote down the words, changing two or three phrases, softening it up just a little.

This is one song I couldn't sing without feeling every minute of it. I still can't. Many a bitch has told me she broke up every time she heard it. So if anybody deserves credit for that, it's Jimmy, I guess – and the others who keep coming home with lipstick on their faces.

When that stops happening, 'Don't explain' will be as dated as the Black Bottom. Until then, it will always be a standard.

I was with Jimmy Monroe for a year before I got wise to something else that was happening. Jimmy smoked something strange. I didn't know for sure until one god-awful night at Mom's place in the Bronx when he got sick.

He was sweating something fierce. Then he'd have the chills and then a fever. Naturally Mom was hovering around wanting to do something to help, wanting to get a doctor. All Jimmy wanted was for her to stay away from him. I tried to explain him to Mom and Mom to him, and Jimmy and I got into one hell of a fight. Then he slapped me.

Mom stepped in and told him not to hit me. Then the three of us got into a bigger fight. Jimmy said he was leaving, and I left with him.

We moved into a hotel first; then we got a little apartment of our own. I was where I wanted to be, with Jimmy. We had our own little place to be happy in. But I wasn't happy. Then Jimmy started letting me lie down with him. My marriage was coming apart. And it was during this time that I got hooked. But one had nothing to do with the other, really, and Jimmy was no more the cause of my doing what I did than my mother was. That goes for any man I ever knew. I was as strong, if not stronger, than any of them. And when it's that way, you can't blame anybody but yourself.

I was working at the Plantation Club in Los Angeles and Jimmy was out there with me when he got into trouble.

Suddenly I was alone and on my own. I had never realized what that would mean. I had to get it myself and didn't know where to begin. I was as helpless as a week-old baby left all alone in its crib, hungry and unable to do anything about it except cry.

I cried until I was sick, exactly the way I had seen Jimmy sick at Mom's apartment on 199th Street. Sick as I was, and alone as I was, I headed back to New York.

Then, the way you always do, I met someone. He was a young boy, fresh up from the South – Alabama or Georgia. He played trumpet and his name was Joseph Luke Guy. He was new on the scene, just getting started as a musician. And he could be a big help to me.

It wasn't long before I was one of the highest-paid slaves around. I was making a thousand a week – but I had about as much freedom as a field hand in Virginia a hundred years before.

Mom was unhappy about me living all alone in a little apartment on 104th Street. It was near her place on 99th Street, but she thought I should stay with her like I always had. I had no husband. Now we had something else in common – both of us were grass widows. She didn't know I had Joe Guy on the string then and I didn't tell her. Finally we compromised and I used to spend three evenings a week with her and the rest with Guy. But that wasn't enough. She was lonely without me and beginning to be real worried about me.

I tried to tell Mama she had the dog, Rajah Ravoy, to take care of her. Rajah was a skinny rundown mutt when Dr Carrington, a West Indian doctor friend of mine, had brought him to me to take care of. He was a sad dog then, and I didn't have time to take care of him so I took him to Mom.

Sometimes when I was working at Café Society I used to take him to work with me. He was so low, I figured he needed the grandest name in the world. So I borrowed the fancy name from a magician who was working a joint in the Village at that time – Rajah Ravoy.

This dog was amazing, he was so smart. In the morning Mom would leave the Bronx and take the bus to 99th Street and Columbus to open her restaurant. Rajah would stand by until she got on the bus, then he'd take off. When she got to the restaurant, there he was, waiting at the door to be fed.

Sometimes he would bark and raise hell and try to keep Mom from going to work in the morning. She knew he was trying to tell her she shouldn't open up that day. And that dog knew what he was doing. She'd stay home and, sure enough, the Board of Health or somebody would be around to make trouble and there was nobody there.

Rajah would go off by himself without any damn leash and go in Central Park to take a bath. The cops and the SPCA people would try to catch him, but he could outwit them any time and come highballing to the apartment, up the stairs. He could do everything, almost ring the bell.

He could even make it all the way from the Bronx to my place on 104th Street. We could have thrown away our telephones, Mom and me. With Rajah we didn't need them.

Mom loved that dog. And the day he died Mom said he was all she had to live for and she wouldn't last long after. And she was so right.

After Joe Guy and I had been together a while we tied up professionally too. We decided I would have my own band and Joe would be the leader. We sure went for the greasy pig when we started that one. But it looked like a big deal in the beginning. I'll never forget the day we went off on the road for the first time. We bought this big beautiful white bus. Painted on the side of it was 'Billie Holiday and her Band.' We were all set to leave; we were supposed to pick up all the cats in the band at the Braddock Hotel on 126th Street, near the stage entrance of the Apollo. It seems like all musicians stayed there. We were all packed up and ready to split when we got a telephone call from Mom.

She wanted to see the bus. 'You can't leave without me seeing your pretty new bus.' So off we detoured to 99th Street. When we got there, Mom invited everybody off the bus to come in and have chicken sandwiches. Then she offered everybody a drink. Then when she got everyone off the bus she had to get in and look it over. Then she started putting up a few fancy little curtains in the back of the bus to dress it up. Then she'd get outside again to see if they were hung straight.

It was the first time out for me and Joe as band leaders and we didn't know enough about it to keep a platoon of Boy Scouts together, let alone grown men. The cats began wandering off to the nearest bar or candy store. I'd get everybody collected, count noses, and find one cat was missing. While I was finding him, two more would sneak away. Anyway, we were three hours behind schedule before we could cut loose from Mom.

I'll always remember her as she stood there on the corner waving to us as we pulled off. Beaming and smiling, she looked like little Miss Five by Five with the most beautiful face you ever saw on a woman.

It was only a few days later in a Washington hotel that I suddenly knew I was alone for good. I don't believe in ghosts or spirits, but I believe what happened that night. We had finished the last show at the Howard Theater and Joe and I went back to our hotel. We were just sitting there when suddenly I felt my mother come up behind me and put her hand on my shoulder. And I knew she was dead.

I turned to Joe. 'Mama just left and she's dead,' I told him.

'You're crazy,' he told me. 'You must be blowing your top.'

'You listen to what I said,' I told him, 'and goddamit you better be good to me because you're all I've got now.'

The next morning when we got to the theater for the first show I could see everybody was ducking me. Our road manager had gotten June Richmond, who has her own club in Paris now, Baby White, and somebody else to stand by and take my place in case I fainted. I saw everybody acting strange, so I just walked up to the road manager and told him Mama was dead and I told him exactly what time she died the night before.

He blew his top, raised hell with everybody backstage. He swore somebody must have told me. But nobody had told me nothing. And everybody knew it.

I came to New York as quick as I could. Joe Glaser had gone ahead and made all the arrangements for the funeral. They brought me to the funeral home, and he came with me. Everybody thought I was terrible because I didn't want to look at Mama in the coffin. Joe insisted that I look at her. The way I felt went way back to Baltimore when my great-grandma had died in my arms; when they made me look at Cousin Ida in her coffin. But Joe Glaser had already put up the money for the embalming and the funeral and he wanted me to realize how much he'd spent on it and how good he'd put her away.

Finally they made me look and see what I didn't want to see. When I did, I really blew my top. She always had lovely clothes, but they had some old kind of an angel-pink lacy shroud on her instead of one of her good suits.

I made them change that. There wasn't anything else I could do. I couldn't cry. When I die people can maybe cry for me because they'll know they're going to start me off in hell and move me from bad to worse. But wherever Mom was going, it couldn't be worse than what she'd known. She was through with trouble, through with heartache, and through with pain.

I went back to Washington and finished the week.

Mom got to be thirty-eight when I was twenty-five. She would never have more than four candles on her birthday cake. So she was only thirty-eight when she died. I'm going to do the same thing. I've staying thirty-eight myself, maybe forty tops. She never cared what the calendars said, and neither do I. Sometimes I feel twenty and sometimes I feel two hundred, and when you do, no arithmetic can pep you up or slow you down.

13

One Never Knows

These were the war years – strange ones for me, too.

My great-grandma had seen the Civil War right outside the windows of her little house on the backside of the Virginia plantation. People like her knew what war was all about, but most of them were dead. The rest of us, what the hell did we know about what was going on.

Parades, War Bond rallies, USO tours, ration books, and letters with weird postmarks, they were far from being the real thing.

I sang to different kinds of audience, saw them change from flannel to khaki, and it always felt like everybody was closer together than before, like we were all stranded in the same big storm. It was like just after an earthquake, everybody talked about the same thing. But it went on so long you got used to it, just like you get used to anything.

I'll never forget the first time I set off on a USO tour, I showed up at the airport all dressed up in a real sharp outfit. I started waltzing up the steps to the Army plane, leading my dog Mister on a real long leash, when suddenly a guy in uniform barked out at me, 'Where do you think you're going, miss?'

'I'm going to Florida to sing and I ain't getting paid, so don't give me no hard time,' I answered him back.

He straightened me out real quick. I had to get down off that stairway, take off my sharp duds, get myself into uniform, leave my dog behind. When I saw the inside of the plane I could see what they were getting at. It was a stripped-down bucket-seated job. You sat on your parachute, staring at somebody else across the way sitting on theirs. By the time you got where you were going you felt like a green recruit who'd spent his first day drilling in the sun.

I don't know how many miles I traveled singing to the troops during those days, by plane, train, even our own white bus. Every time I looked around, Joe Guy had me flying somewhere for a show.

Soldier audiences were so great they spoiled you for the spoiled audiences back home. They loved everything I did, but they never got tired of asking for 'Billie's Blues,' 'Fine and Mellow,' or 'Body and Soul.'

There was nothing you could see more pitiful than a couple of thousand cats, stranded off somewhere in cracker country, with no music, no women, no nothing. After every show they'd pick me to pieces, take the flowers out of my hair and divide them petal by petal. They'd even ask for pieces of my dress, or my stockings even, saying that it had the smell of a woman on it.

Then you'd come back to 52nd Street in New York and find the joint full of cats in khaki. I gave so many going-away parties at the Famous Door and other places, I lost count. It was always the same: three or four young boys would spend the whole night in the joint; we'd lock up, have a final drink, and they'd walk off. A few weeks later I'd get a letter from some damn island somewhere, where they were fighting the bugs and snakes, the heat and the dry rot.

Some of these letters would break your heart. They came from kids I never really knew, or who knew nothing about me, but I was never able to throw them away. Sometimes when they came from kids who really freaked for me, I'd send and get a wind-up victrola and ship it off to them with a bunch of my records or some of Duke Ellington's. These might be rich kids who had everything they wanted in the world back here, and yet when they got an old twenty-dollar victrola and twenty bucks' worth of records they'd think this was the greatest thing that ever happened.

They'd write about waiting and waiting and never knowing for what, going around naked all day and covered up at night to fight off the bugs, and nothing to do except listen to my damn records.

It would be months before they'd see a woman, if ever. Oh, I carried on some torrid long-distance affairs with these kids. Most of them I never saw again. For that I was lucky. The few I did see when they came back tore me apart. One night in the Blue Note in Chicago, late in the war, a kid came in to see me and started talking about a party a couple years before at the Famous Door on 52nd Street. I went along with the gag and the reminiscences and then suddenly I recognized him. His hair had turned completely white and he looked forty years old, though he couldn't have been more than twenty-five when he left.

But none of this stuff was real. Because no man of mine was ever taken away from me by the wars. I don't know what I would have done if he had and some of the things had happened to him like happened to other Negro soldiers.

That stuff ate at you too. So much you didn't know what to do. Negro boys I knew had spent a lifetime scuffling to get up from down South and to make it somewhere in New York. Then bam, they'd be drafted and end up right back in some camp in the South.

Take this cat I knew. He was as nice a guy as you'd want to see, with a wonderful setup in Harlem, a big Cadillac, a fancy apartment, and a beautiful white chick living with him. And all the things that plenty of money could buy.

Within two weeks of the time he kissed this chick goodbye in his Cadillac on Lexington Avenue he was kicking up dust in Georgia. It was his first taste of the South. He didn't even know what he'd been missing.

He almost blew his top. Finally he couldn't take it any more and split for New York. He was AWOL for a week before anyone could even talk to him. You could tell him all the terrible things that were going to happen when they caught up with him, but he could only think about what had already gone down.

Nothing could be worse than this. Finally his girl and me got so nervous we put through a call to the first sergeant of his outfit in Georgia. We told him our problem. He said they hadn't even missed him yet, but something was up. The CO was on his trail. If he split right back, his topkick said, they might not ever know he'd been gone. With this we were able to convince him to go back and face the music.

And music it was, too. By Irving Berlin. When he got back they rushed him off to audition as a dancer for a part in *This Is the Army*. He spent the rest of the damn war in his tap shoes, with his chick following him from town to town.

Then there were others. When I think of kids like Jimmy Davis I could cry to think of all the life and talent we lost in the damn war and that nobody even knows about. Jimmy was in the Army when he wrote 'Lover Man' and brought it straight to me.

I loved it and wanted to record it. Before I could do it he had been shipped off to Europe and I never saw him again. He's got to be dead.

I took the song to Milt Gabler at Decca and I went on my knees to him, I loved it so. I didn't want to do it with the ordinary six pieces. I begged Milt and told him I had to have strings behind me. I think Milt Gabler had got in solid at Decca on account of me and my recording of 'Strange Fruit,' but I had to crawl to get that song recorded, and recorded right. Ram Ramirez gets all the credit for 'Lover Man,' but that's only part of the story.

People don't understand the kind of fight it takes to record what you want to record the way you want to record it. I've fought as long as ten years to get to record a song I loved or wanted to do. Plenty of times people come to me with material. I like it, I tell them I like it, and then nothing happens. I've still got songs I'm fighting to record.

Sometimes it's worse to win a fight than to lose. Because if you win and the song comes out and it dies, the recording people hold that over your head for years and beat you out of having your way.

Something like that happened with 'Some Other Spring.' It was a beautiful song and it had Irene Wilson's heartbreak over Teddy written all over it. She was a famous pianist herself, and John Hammond had spotted her long before either of them saw Teddy. He was a boy when she met him, taught him, and married him. Later Teddy fell for her best friend across the hall and left Irene. Poor Renie almost died. I was out with her one night and Benny Webster and Kenny Klook Clarke, trying to cheer her up. There was a damn noisy radiator going in the restaurant, and when somebody said the radiator noise sounded like a melody we began kidding about it, and the next thing we knew we had a song. Arthur Herzog and Danny Mendelsohn got into the act before we were through, and I took it finally to Benny Goodman.

Benny liked it. In fact he said it was too beautiful, it wouldn't sell. Everything right then had to be hot and jumping. Benny said nobody would buy it. But I went ahead and recorded it anyway. He was right. It didn't sell.

I guess 'Travelin' Light' was one of my biggest-selling records. It happened on the West Coast in 1944. Trummy Young, that great trombone player, was about to get thrown out of his Los Angeles hotel for the usual reason. So was I. Both of us might have been thinking about traveling light via the fire escape or something when Jimmy Mundy, the arranger, approached me and asked if I'd like to do the number with Paul Whiteman's band.

Sure, I told Jimmy, I'd be glad to.

Trummy had actually written the tune. I had worked on it just a little to make it right for me.

The same day I recorded it with Whiteman's band, Johnny Mercer and Martha Tilton were around recording the same tune. From that, we thought we were really going to hit it big. Trummy got seventy-five dollars for the tune and I got the same for singing it.

We took that loot, paid our rent, went out and celebrated, had some Chinese food, and wound up only five bucks ahead of where we'd been at the start. I had to wire Mom for carfare so Trummy and I could grab a bus and make it back East.

Trummy and I never got another quarter. Royalties were still unheard of. I didn't know there was such a thing.

14

I'm Pulling Through

I spent the rest of the war on 52nd Street and a few other streets. I had the white gowns and the white shoes. And every night they'd bring me the white gardenias and the white junk.

When I was on, I was on and nobody gave me any trouble. No cops, no Treasury agents, nobody.

I got into trouble when I tried to get off.

Along about the end of the war I went to Joe Glaser's office and told him I wanted to kick and I'd need help. I went to my boss at the Famous Door on 52nd Street, Tony Golucci, and I told him. Tony had been Mr Wonderful to me before, but he was so good to me at that time I hope God will bless him all his days. I didn't say a word to another soul.

Tony kept my job open. He offered to backstop me with the money I needed. But it was the way he did it I'll never forget, with love and respect, like a human being holding out his hand to someone who needed it.

We looked for the best private sanatorium around. Money was no object. Finally the one we were recommended to turned out to be right in Manhattan. They promised to take me. And the price was two thousand dollars for three weeks' stay. This was daylight robbery, sure. But it was cheap, too, if my stay there and the treatment were guaranteed confidential. And it was.

Joe and Tony told everybody I'd had a nervous breakdown. There were so many of those happening, everybody was happy to believe it. We set the date. I checked in.

It took almost three weeks. Joe Glaser sent me flowers and things. But I was happy when it was over. I was sure I'd make it. I was ready to go back to work; my job was waiting. This was my first try at going straight on my own, and I was sure it would work out.

I walked down the steps of the sanatorium. A cab was waiting for me, and Miss Church, Joe Glaser's secretary. Before I could get in, my hopes sank to despair. I saw a man there and I knew he was from the law and I knew he was trailing me.

I couldn't believe it. Nobody knew I was there but Joe and Tony. I knew they hadn't told a soul. The word must have come from the hospital. I felt like going back there and busting the place up. It had cost me two thousand dollars to be sure the whole deal was absolutely confidential. It would have been curtains for me as a public performer if it had gotten out. I trusted the doctors and nurses. I had to. And somebody had betrayed me. Why? Who?

I was so panicked then I didn't think about it.

But I've thought about it a lot since. And I've had plenty of time.

Back in the 1920s there was a big scandal in New York involving the cops and the Federal Narcotics Bureau. A bunch of guys were busted when it was discovered they had a racket going on. The cops and Feds would put the pinch on wealthy drug addicts. They would threaten to arrest them then they would let them off, provided these people agreed to go to a private sanatorium the fuzz recommended and take the 'cure.' So these rich people went for it. They went to places like I had gone to, paid the same kind of money I paid, and then the detectives got a big commission.

There was a shake-up in the police department and the Narcotics Bureau, and that crap was supposed to have been stopped. But crap like that never stops.

These sanatoriums depend on the law to stay in business. They can be closed up overnight, but tight, if the Narcotics Bureau wants to.

The relations between a doctor and his patient are supposed to be confidential. I trusted those doctors and nurses. And one of them had betrayed me. Maybe the law just came busting in, asking questions, and somebody squawked. Maybe the law just shadows the hospital all the time to pick up likely prospects and then goes and busts them. I don't know.

All I know is that when I was on nobody bothered me, no laws, no cops, no federal agents. And nobody tailed me. I didn't get heated up until I made an honest-to-God sincere effort to kick. Whoever did that to me changed the whole course of my life. I'll never forgive them.

It's tough enough coming off when you've got someone who loves you and trusts you and believes in you. I didn't have anybody. No family, no man who loved me. I had nobody but Tony Golucci and Joe Glaser who would believe in me.

And against them there was the law, betting their time, their shoe leather, and their money that they would get me. Nobody can live like that.

15

The Same Old Story

If you're an American citizen and unless you go to bed early these nights, you're liable to see me on the late-late show in a movie I made in Hollywood in 1946. It was my first Hollywood picture. My latest, too.

I was working in a Hollywood club when Joe Glaser made the deal. It was an independent picture, produced by Jules Levey, called *New Orleans* and supposedly about it.

I thought I was going to play myself in it. I thought I was going to be Billie Holiday doing a couple of songs in a nightclub setting and that would be that.

I should have known better. When I saw the script, I did. You just tell me one Negro girl who's made movies who didn't play a maid or a whore. I don't know any. I found out I was going to do a little singing, but I was still playing the part of a maid.

I was sore at Joe Glaser for signing me for the part. I'd fought my whole life to keep from being somebody's damn maid. And after making more than a million bucks and establishing myself as a singer who had some taste and self respect, it was a real drag to go to Hollywood and end up as a make-believe maid.

Don't get me wrong. I've got nothing against maids – or whores – whether they're black or white. My mother was a maid, a good one, one of the greatest. My step-mother is Tallulah Bankhead's maid right now, and that's a part I'd even consider when they do her life story. I've been what I've been. But I don't think I'm the type for maid parts; I don't feel it. I didn't feel this damn part. How could I, after going through hell to keep from being one when I was twelve?

So I began to heckle Joe Glaser on the long-distance telephone, telling him I wasn't going to play Topsy, not for all the Bank of America's loot, bad as I needed it. But he warned me that if I walked out on the contract I'd signed it would play hell for me. I'd never work in Hollywood again.

So the scuffle at the studio began. They sent me to a dramatic coach on the lot to coach me in my lines. My name was Miz Lindy in the thing. And about the only lines I had called for me to say, 'Yez, Miss Marylee. No, Miss Marylee,' in twenty-three different kinds of ways. So this coach was trying to brief me on how to get the right kind of Tom feeling into this thing.

A Mexican cat by the name of Arturo de Cordova played the gambler hero; Irene Rich played this girl's mother; she was sweet and nice as could be off camera, but in the picture she had to carry on with all the Dixieland stuff.

Louis Armstrong played Louis, and with him in his group were Zutty Singleton, Kid Ory, Barney Bigard, Bud Scott, Red Calendar, and Charlie Beal. Meade Lux Lewis also did a Chicago bit in the thing, and even Woody Herman got in it. And I was supposed to be the maid of the family and also Louis' girl friend on the side. One of those kind of deals.

The first time I got on the set with a black floor-length outfit on and a little white cap, they had the lights set up, the cameramen were worrying, the grips were kicking up a storm, assistant directors working like beavers, make-up men dusting you off, hairdressers messing with your wig, and then came the big moment for me to say, 'Yez, Miss Marylee.'

I swallowed hard and said it. The director hollered 'Cut!' right off. He said I definitely didn't say the name of Miss Marylee correctly.

'Nobody, but nobody in New Orleans talks like that,' he said.

'All right,' I said, 'I can say it any damn way you want.' So I gave him 'Miss Marylee' about fifty different ways until he was dizzy.

When working with the coach I had practiced saying 'Miss Marylee' all day, when I finally said to her, 'Tell me, girl, who the hell is this Miss Marylee?'

They flipped. She was only the star of this particular picture.

I never did set very well with women. This chick must have

been from somewhere South or on the border. Some people don't actually love Negroes and don't want to make love to them, but they don't actually hate them neither. This girl wasn't one of those. She wanted nothing to do with me.

You can see this picture today on TV and still see it in those scenes I played with her. Every night after we'd finished work at six o'clock, Blondie would rush to the projection room to see the rushes and find out how she was doing. I didn't have time to look at no rushes; I had to rush myself off to the club, where I'd work all night, and then rush back to get there by 6 AM, get made up, and be on the set.

After the 'star' looked at a few days' rushes she decided I was stealing scenes from her. This was a laugh. I was no actress, never had been one, never pretended to be one. I hadn't done any acting since I used to play *True Story* serials on the radio with Shelton Brooks back in the thirties. But when this girl said 'Frog,' all the people on the set would jump. So they had to convince her they were helping her keep me from stealing the picture.

But unlike her, I got along fine with the cameramen. I dug from the beginning these were the most important cats around. They're like the boys in the control room when you're making records. You can turn in the best performance in the world, but if those cats in the control room aren't with you when they turn those little knobs or twist those little dials, you might just as well have stayed in bed, Jack. So it was with the cameramen. You could be acting up a storm that would blow an Oscar your way, and if those cats on the cameras aren't with you, you're nowhere.

I kept calling Joe Glaser every day, and I worked all night every night. Finally one day on the set I took about all I could from Blondie. I was tired of her giving me a hard time. They had me cornered. I couldn't walk off like I wanted to. So I bust out crying.

This time Louis Armstrong blew the whistle.

'Better look out,' he said to the director and the producer and the actors on the set. 'I know Lady, and when she starts crying, the next thing she's going to do is start fighting.'

Anyway, the picture was finished some kind of way and I was

glad to split the hell out of there and be gone. I saw it later, much later – and found out Blondie must have had her way. They had taken miles of footage of music and scenes in New Orleans, but none of it was left in the picture. And very damn little of me. I know I wore a white dress for a number I did in the picture. And all that was cut out of the picture.

I never made another movie. And I'm in no hurry.

By the time the picture opened on Broadway I was already far from the scene. I never got to read what the critics said about it until just now. Most of them were rough on the picture – almost as rough as they should have been. Some of them were kind to me, maybe kinder than they should have been.

Archer Winsten, bless him, reported that my singing in the picture retained 'the personal style that has inspired countless imitators. It is good to be able to say that some portion of her vocal and emotional sincerity makes itself felt on the screen at the very time she herself is in sad circumstances.'

You got to be sharp to look between the scenes of that picture and smell the hassle that went on.

But any hassle like that is worth what it cost me, if just one person can look at the end result and dig what you'd been trying to do.

16

Too Hot for Words

Trouble is a thing I've learned to smell.

And I smelled it for sure that night in May 1947 when we closed at the Earle Theater in Philadelphia. It was almost a year since I left that private sanatorium in New York clean – and the law had been tailing me on and off ever since, from New York to Hollywood and back. They were around in Chicago when we worked there.

And then they picked us up the week we were booked at the Earle Theater on the same bill with Louis Armstrong and his group. We had come down from New York in a hired car – me and Joe Guy, Bobby Tucker, my accompanist, and Jimmy Asundio, a young fellow who was then my road manager. Joe went back to New York early in the week, and the rest of us were going to drive back to New York with the car and the chauffeur. After the last show something told me not to go back to the hotel.

If they're going to bust you, they always try to wait and do it after you've closed. If somebody is pinched in the middle of the week, club owners and theater managers have a fit; they complain the publicity gives their place a bad name and stuff like that. And the cops are usually very considerate of their feelings. But as soon as your last show is over you're on the street and all bets are off.

I begged Bobby and Jimmy not to go back to the hotel. But they wouldn't listen to me. They had left things in their room. Some of my clothes and make-up were in my room. They wanted to go back and pack up. I learned to trust my hunches. I told them to leave it. We could call the hotel later and they would send the stuff on to New York.

But they laughed at me and my hunches and went on ahead to the hotel. When I had finished taking off my make-up and getting into something comfortable I left the theater, and the hired chauffeur drove me to the hotel to pick up the boys. My dog Mister was in the back seat.

When we pulled up in front of the hotel I knew I was right. I could see through the windows. The lobby was full of cops. Quickly I told the chauffeur to pull around the corner. From the way he reacted, I could tell he wasn't going to be any help. It's awful to be in trouble with someone who doesn't have the heart for it.

We stopped around the corner, and then I saw a federal agent cross the street and come towards us. He was an Indian chap. I recognized him. I had never driven a car in my life before. But that didn't matter. I knew I had to do it that night and there wasn't two seconds to waste taking any lessons.

I hollered to the chauffeur to get out from behind the wheel and leave the motor running. As the Treasury agent came towards us, I stepped on the gas. He hollered 'Halt!' and tried to stop the car by standing in the road. But I kept driving right on and he moved. I pulled away through a rain of bullets.

My boxer dog Mister was in the back seat whimpering, scared. And the chauffeur was in the front seat the same way. I didn't listen or stop for nothing. I knew I couldn't do anything to help Bobby and Jimmy unless I could make it to New York. And I couldn't make it to New York unless I kept my head and kept my nose on the road. I figured they might try to barricade the streets in Philly somewhere, so I made the chauffeur show me how to go over the river and come up through Camden, New Jersey. I'll never know how I made it, but I made it.

This was Friday. I was scheduled to open at the Onyx Club on 52nd Street the next night. First I had to get a lawyer. Bobby was as innocent as a babe; he never used nothing; he didn't even drink. He'd go to parties and have a glass of pop and have a ball, thinking he was loaded like everybody else.

I got Bobby out of jail and he joined me. He told me that a couple of federal agents had come to their room in the hotel, walked in without a warrant or anything, and searched the place. They said they found the 'evidence' under the bed.

I opened at the Onyx and nothing happened. They didn't even come around until the third night. They hung around from then on. And they let me work the full week. It's always that way. While they were trying to get a case against me they were also doing the management a favor by not busting me on the premises.

But I knew they would try and get me again when the week was over. I was sick. I had been tailed for a year and I couldn't face having it go on like that forever. I knew I could never kick again, and stay kicked, as long as they were after me. I could try. But that would take money. It had cost two thousand dollars before. It would probably cost as much now. And I couldn't get it together without Joe Glaser's help.

With my salary from the Philly week, plus the Onyx week, I could afford to get admitted to the best hospital in the country. Without it, they could hunt me down like a dog and send me to jail. Joe Glaser told me this was the best thing that could happen to me. And I had nowhere else to turn.

When I finished the week at the Onyx, I took a cab to the Hotel Grampion. Two agents were waiting for me in the lobby with a warrant for my arrest. They walked me to my room. Joe Guy was waiting there. The door was locked when we got there. While the Treasury agents knocked, I hollered, 'Joe, it's the fuzz, clean up.'

They arrested both of us and took us off, him to New York and me to Philadelphia. Most of my belongings, gowns, clothes, jewelry, were stolen from the hotel before Bobby Tucker could come back and claim them.

Most federal agents are nice people. They've got a dirty job to do and they have to do it. Some of the nicer ones have feeling enough to hate themselves sometime for what they have to do. But they don't have anything more to say about the laws than me. They just got to take orders. They're not like some city cops, nasty and wrong. Federal agents will get a doctor for you; they don't want you around sick and throwing up, or worse, on their hands.

Maybe they would have been kinder to me if they'd been nasty; then I wouldn't have trusted them enough to believe what they told me. While I was in their hands they gave me decent food, always kept me in someone's office while they questioned me. I was never behind bars the whole time. I've seen a federal judge bawl out one of them when they brought a sick man into court. He said to take the man to a doctor, get him out of there. That's better than they're allowed to do under the law. Under the law they have got to treat sick people like criminals. But they treat them like sick people, too, whenever they can.

It reminded me of Welfare Island. If someone's got eyes for you, it's easier for them to treat you like a human being. The matron at Welfare Island was nice to me and saved my life because she was on the make. Philly. I wasn't too much of a drug addict for some of these federal men not to make passes at me. And it was the same way at the Federal Building. They might not speak to me in the street, but they'd gladly sleep with me in the Federal Building.

17

Don't Know if I'm Coming or Going

It was called 'The United States of America versus Billie Holiday.' And that's just the way it felt.

They brought me into a courtroom in the US District Courthouse at Ninth and Market streets in Philly – only two blocks from the Earle Theater where it had all begun eleven days before. But those two damn blocks seemed like the Atlantic Ocean. It was Tuesday, May 27, 1947.

Somebody read off the charge: 'On or about May 16, 1947, and divers dates theretofore in the Eastern District of Pennsylvania, Billie Holiday, did receive, conceal, carry and facilitate the transportation and concealment of . . . drugs . . . fraudulently imported and brought into the United States contrary to law, in violation of Section 174, Title 21, U.S.C.A.'

An assistant US district attorney opened. 'All right, Billie Holiday,' he said. 'You are charged with violation of the Narcotics Act and you have been shown a copy of the information and have indicated your desire to waive the presentation of an indictment by the Grand Jury. You are entitled to a lawyer.'

'I have none,' I said. And that was the truth. I hadn't seen one, talked to one.

'Do you want a lawyer, Miss Holiday?' the D.A. asked.

'No,' I answered.

I didn't think there was anyone who would help me. And worse, I had been convinced that nobody *could* help me.

'Then this is a waiver of appointment of counsel if you will sign "Billie Holiday" on that line.'

They shoved me a pink paper to sign and I signed it.

I would have signed anything, no matter what. I hadn't eaten anything for a week. I couldn't even keep water down. Every time I tried to take a nap, some big old officer would come around and wake me up to sign something, make me dress, go to another office.

When it came time for me to appear in court I couldn't even walk. I was in no shape to go before the judge. So they agreed to give me a shot to keep me from getting sick. It turned out to be morphine.

Then the judge spoke up. 'Was this woman ever represented by counsel?' he asked.

The district attorney replied, 'I had a call today from a man who had been her counsel, and I explained the matter to him and then he returned a call and stated they were not interested in coming down and wanted the matter handled as it is being handled now.'

I can read that sentence today and weep. 'They were not interested in coming down and wanted the matter handled as it is being handled.' In plain English that meant that no one in the world was interested in looking out for me at this point.

If a woman drowns her baby, about the worst thing you can do, she's still got a right to see a lawyer, and I'd help get her one if I could.

I couldn't very well expect the Legal Aid Society to come rushing in to help a chick making a couple thousand a week or more. I knew I was on my own. Glaser had told me this before. 'Girl,' he said, 'this is the best thing that could happen to you.'

I needed to go to a hospital and he was telling me the woodshed would be better.

So they handed me a white paper to sign. 'This is a waiver of presentation of an indictment to the Grand Jury, Miss Holiday.' They never had it so easy. I signed the second paper. The rest was up to them. I was just a pigeon.

'How do you plead?' said the clerk.

'I would like to plead guilty and be sent to a hospital,' I said.

Then the D.A. spoke up. 'If Your Honor please, this is a case of a drug addict, but more serious, however, than most of our cases, Miss Holiday is a professional entertainer and among the higher rank as far as income is concerned. She has been in Philadelphia

and appeared at the Earle Theater, where she had a week's engagement; our agents in the Narcotics Bureau were advised from our
Chicago office that she was a heroin addict and undoubtedly had
heroin on her.'

'The Chicago office advised you?' the judge asked.

'That is right,' the D.A. replied. 'She had previously been in Chicago on an engagement. They checked and found that when she
left the Earle Theater or prepared to leave the Earle Theater, prior
to leaving she had in her possession some capsules . . . and trans-
ferred them to a man who was supposed to be her manager, named
James Asundio.

'Subsequent to that, while James Asundio and Bobby Tucker
were packing the bags, the agents came and identified themselves
and told them why they were there, and Asundio said it was his
room. They made a search of the room with his permission and
found some capsules wrapped in a package of silk lining.

'Subsequently, Miss Holiday was apprehended in New York,' he
went on. 'She has given these agents a full and complete statement
and came in here last week with the booking agent (Glaser) and
expressed a desire to be cured of this addiction. Very unfortunately
she has had following her the worst type of parasites and leeches
you can think of. We have learned that in the past three years she
has earned almost a quarter of a million dollars, but last year it was
$56,000 or $57,000, and she doesn't have any of that money.

'These fellows who have been traveling with her,' this young
D.A. continued melodramatically, 'would go out and get these
drugs and would pay five and ten dollars and they would charge
her one hundred and two hundred dollars for the same amount of
drugs. It is our opinion that the best thing that can be done for her
would be to put her in a hospital where she will be properly treated
and perhaps cured of this addiction.'

Then the judge took over. He asked my age, if I was married,
how long I'd been separated from my husband, if we had any kids,
where he worked, my life story, my show-business history.

He asked me if I didn't know it was 'wrong' to have possession
of narcotics. What did he expect me to say? I told him I couldn't

help it after I started. Then he asked how much I used. When the federal agent Roder told him, the judge wanted to know if this was a large amount. Roder told him it was enough to kill either of them. They wouldn't be dead, they'd be damn high, that's all.

Then he wanted to know how many grains I had started with. Hell, I was no more of a pharmacist than he was. I was sick of grown men getting their kicks out of all this. They had told me if I pleaded guilty they'd send me to a hospital. I was sick and wanted to get there. This wasn't getting anyone anywhere.

I broke in and spoke to the judge. 'I'm willing to go to the hospital, Your Honor,' I said.

'I know,' he said, brushing me off.

'I want the cure,' I told him.

'You stand here indicted criminally as a user of narcotics,' he said, looking me in the eye. Then the judge and the federal agents got into a long hassle which had nothing to do with me either. The chief of the Philadelphia bureau stepped up and gave the judge a lecture on how hard they were working and said, 'I am only saying very little, if any, good will be served with her indictment and conviction other than her individual interest if we do not get some lead as to the source.'

The judge seemed to be saying they were doing me a favor. And he kept talking about an indictment and conviction, but there was nobody there to object.

Then the judge started on me again, asking me where I'd been on tour, who was with me, how much money I made, and where it was. This might have gone on forever except that somebody came in, went into a huddle with the judge. He must have been a probation officer or a social worker or something.

Then the judge lowered the boom.

'I want you to understand, as I intimated at the time of your plea, that you stand here as a criminal defendant, and while your plight is rather pitiful, we have no doubt but that you, having been nine years associated in the theatrical world, pretty well appreciate what is right – and your experiences have been many, I have been led to understand.

'I want you to know you are being committed as a criminal defendant; you are not being sent to a hospital alone primarily for treatment. You will get treatment, but I want you to know you stand convicted as a wrongdoer. Any other wrongdoer who has associated with you is a matter that is not for our consideration now.

'In your imprisonment you are going to find that you are going to get the very best medical treatment which can be accorded to you. That is the beneficial part of the government's position in this case.

'I do not think you have told the whole truth about your addiction at all . . . Your commitment will depend largely on yourself, that of the supervisor and the government generally, and we hope that within the time limit in which you are to serve you will rehabilitate yourself and return to society a useful individual and take your place in the particular calling which you have chosen and in which you have been successful.

'The sentence of the court is that you undergo imprisonment for a period of one year and one day. The Attorney General will designate the prison in which the incarceration will be made.'

It was all over in a matter of minutes; they gave me another shot to keep me from getting sick on the train, and at nine o'clock that night I was in an upper berth on a train headed for the Federal Woman's Reformatory at Alderson, West Virginia, with two big fat white matrons guarding me.

They acted as though they were scared to death of me. When I asked one of them to get me a bottle of beer she gasped and told me it was against regulations. Hell, I had a package of stuff to keep me from getting sick. That was against regulations too. Except nobody wanted to take a chance of letting me get deadly sick on the train. Finally one matron gave up and went and got me one little old bottle of beer.

But the Philadelphia story wasn't over. They started bringing me back from Alderson to Philly to question me and question me. I hated that. They brought me up so often, the girls at the place began to think I was a stool pigeon. And there's no place worse than the

Philadelphia jail where they used to keep me. It's worse than Welfare Island, damp all the time, with rats in it big as my Chihuahua. There were women there with TB and worse, doing life terms for murder and stuff, and I had to eat with them and sleep with them.

When they weren't finding out what they thought I knew, the Treasury agent fixed it so I'd arrive at the Philly jail on Friday night and have to lay over in that hellhole until Monday before I was questioned. Talk about your brainwashings, I've had it.

What made it worse was they brought me up when they tried Jimmy Asundio and again later when they tried Joe Guy. Both of them stood on their legal rights, had good lawyers, and both of them got off. Jimmy's conviction was reversed by a higher court because the federal agents had come into his room without a warrant. And Joe Guy was acquitted by a jury in a few minutes. They had no case; the judge told them so, and the jury agreed.

I felt like the fool of all time.

People on drugs are sick people. So now we end up with the government chasing sick people like they were criminals, telling doctors they can't help them, prosecuting them because they had some stuff without paying the tax, and sending them to jail.

Imagine if the government chased sick people with diabetes, put a tax on insulin and drove it into the black market, told doctors they couldn't treat them, and then caught them, prosecuted them for not paying their taxes, and then sent them to jail. If we did that, everyone would know we were crazy. Yet we do practically the same thing every day in the week to sick people hooked on drugs. The jails are full and the problem is getting worse every day.

18

Travelin' All Alone

If I had known what kind of 'cure' I was in for at Alderson, I could have taken it alone – just locking myself in a room and throwing away the key.

There was no cure. They don't cut you down slow, weaning you off the stuff gradually. They just throw you in the hospital by yourself, take you off cold turkey, and watch you suffer.

The first nights I was ready to quit. I thought I'd just explode. But after a while it passes just like everything else, after you've been through hell.

If anybody ever got anything into a federal prison, I want to hear all about it. After they're through putting their fingers up to there, taking out your bridgework, X-raying your stomach, there's no way in the world to get anything in there.

For the first few days it's just like the Army. You're in quarantine and they test you from top to toe; smear tests, blood tests, skin tests, eye tests, IQ tests, aptitude tests for jobs. Then after twenty-five days of this you get to take a look at the place.

It's out in the country, six cottages with fifty to sixty girls in each one. But it's completely Jim Crow; three cottages for white girls, three for colored. That goes for sleeping and eating. As for working, white and black get to put on the harness side by side. And when you march to and from work, it's one formation for the Negroes and one for the ofays. The chapel was Jim Crow; white girls pray in front, black girls in back. In the movies it was the same deal.

With all that, the place wasn't too bad. A hell of a big improvement over Welfare Island, for one thing. If you're real good, you get to go to classes in Spanish, woodcraft, cooking, ceramics, and stuff like that. If you're real great, you can get to go to six classes a week, if you're not beat from working so hard. Later I made a lot of jewelry and stuff in ceramics class and brought it back with me.

When I came out of quarantine I went to work on the farm, picking tomatoes and other vegetables. I had seen worms and bugs before but didn't have no dealing with them, and I was still scared of those devils. But I guess they figured outside work was what I needed after I came off my habit. One day I passed out with the sunstroke from working in the heat. So they sent me to the hospital and the doctor gave me some more tests. Finally the doctor told them I was a city girl and ought to have some kind of damn job inside. But nothing happened, and nobody lays off work there unless you are sick, and you've got to be able to prove it.

Quite a few girls, especially long-termers in the joint, were lovers and would take these farm jobs so they could be together when they worked. It was still impossible for them to get together to do anything, but they could pass notes and exchange valentines and stuff. The only real chance girls had to get together was coming back from the movies. This was the only time they didn't make the girls march in Jim Crow formation. It was after dark usually, and black and white could mix a little. This was the only chance lovers had to hold hands or anything.

After all those intelligence tests, IQ tests, and aptitude tests, they gave me my second job, in the piggery, as a maid for a herd of damn dirty squealing pigs. I'd never seen a pig before in my damn life, and you know my IQ isn't as bad as all that. Maybe somebody figured I was a celebrity, so they had to bend over backwards so nobody would think they were doing me any favors.

That joint grows every bit of food they use the year round, except the turkeys and some other things we got for Thanksgiving and Christmas.

One day I got so sick of hearing those squealing-ass pigs, I crawled up on the roof of the pigsty and went sound asleep. I might have slept there all day, but suddenly I heard the sirens blowing, and it woke me up and I walked back to the cottage. When I got there everybody started grabbing me, asking where I'd been, saying they were looking all over for me. Two girls had escaped a week or so before.

'Where the hell you think I've been?' I said. 'Sleeping on the roof, and now I'm going to my room.'

'Oh no, you're not,' they said, 'you're in trouble.'

And I was, too. I was put in seclusion and lost my cigarette privileges. It was like the cooler at Welfare Island, only not so bad. You got your three meals a day, but you're still locked up all by yourself, and that's hell for me. The prison doctor knew it and got me out after four days. He knew I had claustrophobia and he reminded them I was a city girl. 'There must be something this girl can do,' he told them.

After all the big personnel experts got together to figure out a job that was right for a city girl like me, I was cast for the part of Cinderella of Cottage No. 6. This was nothing but a fairy-tale name for permanent K.P. I worked in the cottage kitchen as a handy gal and helper. It was my job to wash the dishes, clean the windows, bring up the coal – no gas there in the country, nothing but a big coal-eating stove – lay the fires in the evening with papers and stuff ready for the morning.

By the time my chores were over in the evening, the recreation time was over and it was time for bed. Then I had to be up at five in the morning, have the dining room open, the tables laid, the cereal cooked, the milk poured into glasses, the bread counted off in slices, the water poured, and the coffee made.

And although they grew all their own food on the grounds, they treated it like it was money in the bank. Man, every carrot was counted. You were given just enough for one portion for each girl in the cottage – no more, no less. If the census changed one day, so did the food ration. If you messed up, having too much or too little, you had to pay – the only way it mattered – by losing your cigarettes for a day or a week, depending on how serious a jam you were in.

I always caught hell over the coffee. I always made it too good, and the supply ran out before it was supposed to.

I used to steal food for the girls, too, but I never got caught for that. Especially those girls who were just coming off a habit. When you're kicking, you get what we call the chucks, and after that you're hungry all the time.

I never did get the chucks while I was kicking. I guess I was too busy thinking about 'the street' all the time and the life I'd left. But the girls that had them really suffered. They'd leave the table so hungry they'd cry all night. I would steal grub for them and they'd take it in their rooms, hide it in their mattresses or wherever they could. Sometimes they'd get caught and busted, but nobody ever squealed.

Being Cinderella was a hard job, especially the part that called for carrying up twelve buckets of coal every night. But I never minded any part of it except the last chore at night, which was locking the cottage door. As soon as that door slammed locked, I would start thinking about being locked in that Catholic institution with the body of a dead girl, and my back would begin to crawl. I didn't mind anything much except that locked door.

During my months in the joint they told me I was receiving packs of mail every day. It gave me a terrific kick to know people remembered me. At Christmas time especially I got over three thousand cards from every state in the Union and from towns like Shanghai, Bombay, Cape Town, and Alexandria as well as all over Europe.

But I couldn't get any of my mail because the rule book says you are only allowed to get letters from your immediate family. And death had done me fresh out of immediate family. There was nobody left. Pop and Mom were dead. If there had been anybody, believe me, those federal social workers would have found them. Those people are thorough.

I had a white half sister and brother somewhere – the ones I met at Pop's funeral. But they had vanished into the ofay world without a trace. Everybody was dead except my stepmother, Fanny Holiday, and my cousins Henry and Elsie. Neither of them were considered immediate family.

And the stuff people sent that I couldn't touch! Fruit, wine, whisky, champagne. I loved them for it, but they had to send it back.

A wonderful couple in Zurich, Switzerland, sent me a thousand dollars and a telegram telling me that America would never accept me again when I got out, so I should come to them in Europe. They telephoned me twice from Europe and the warden was nice enough to let me speak to them. I told them I couldn't run away; maybe they were right and America wouldn't accept me. But I had to find out for myself. I had the warden, Mrs Helen Hironimus, send the thousand dollars back, and I told them if I didn't make it when I got out I'd call on them to send me the money and I'd come over. 'But I think I can make it,' I told them.

The warden didn't have to let me talk to these friends from Europe. And she didn't have to let me receive any mail from friends, but she finally decided I could get my three letters a week from people besides my family. The ones selected were Bobby Tucker, my faithful accompanist, and Ed Fishman, a fellow who wanted to be my manager when I got out. Fishman used to call the warden every day. And since the warden wanted to do everything she could about helping me to make a comeback when I got out, she let me talk to Fishman and Joe Glaser.

The warden was a real nice chick. She was a fine woman. She had money and didn't have to work at a job like that. She did it because she believed in what she was doing. After church on Sundays she would always come by the hospital where the girls were kicking dope. That's the first time I saw her, on one of those visits. When you're lying there in torment, counting the minutes, the last thing you want to see is a pretty woman, and warden Helen Hironimus was a pretty one. But she knew and didn't let that stop her. She'd bring flowers and give them to the girls having a rough time. After a few days you get to thinking she's kind of sharp. Then you discover yourself liking the dame.

I didn't sing a note the whole time I was in Alderson. I didn't feel like singing. So I didn't. A lot of the girls in there were nice kids. They used to beg me to perform and they'd get sore at me when I refused. It didn't matter. I couldn't have sung if I'd wanted to. If they'd understood my kind of singing they'd have known I couldn't sing in a place like that. The whole basis of my singing is feeling.

Unless I feel something, I can't sing. In the whole time I was there I didn't feel a thing.

The girls used to give those goddamn amateur shows. Even the warden asked if I wouldn't participate. I gave her the same answer. I told her I had been sent there to be punished and that was that, and nothing to sing about. I went to the first show the kids gave. It was Halloween and some of the girls were dressed up as boys, carrying on on stage the way they couldn't off stage.

It was absolutely disgusting and so depressing I never went back to see any of their damn amateur nights. This made everybody mad. But they'd still play my records. People must have sent me more than five hundred of my recordings while I was in there, and I left them there. I seldom listened to my own records outside, so I didn't in there, either.

When it got near to Christmas of 1947 in the joint, I was determined to have some whisky some kind of way. I had the run of the kitchen and I figured, if anybody could do it, it was up to me. I remembered the Chinese laundryman in Baltimore, Mr Lee, and the handmade whisky he used to make out of rice.

I was afraid to steal the rice. I was sure they'd miss it and catch up with me. So I figured I would pull off the same effect by using potato peelings. Even that was tricky. For doing something as petty as peeling potatoes too thick, you caught hell. But I managed to get the peelings together and I soon had a mess of whisky so good you could smell it working. But that was just the beginning of the trouble. The smell was so potent I had hell hiding that stuff.

The more it fermented, the more it stank. I tried every place to hide it, under the woodpile, behind the stove, in my room. And the warden tried just as many places looking for the stuff. She was no damn fool. She could smell the stuff. But by this time the smell was all over the joint.

She figured something must have crawled in somewhere and died. So she made me clean the joint immaculate. There was nobody working in the kitchen but me and a woman who was sixty-five years old, so she figured it had to be one of us doing the bootlegging.

Finally the warden got around to looking in the last place I had hid it – underneath the coal pile. For this I lost my cigarettes for two weeks, and all that great whisky too.

After your first five months in the joint you get assigned to a beautiful room with a hospital-type bed – not soft, not hard, but O.K. You had one comfortable chair and one straight chair. They let you buy material, if you got the loot, to make drapes and slip covers for the bed. But you have to keep the whole joint clean, waxing the floors and everything. When inspection time comes, one of the matrons comes around with a white glove on her hand, and there better not be any dust on anything, or puff, there go those cigarettes again.

The only thing they had in the joint that I cared about was cigarettes. When I went in I was at the point where I smoked almost a carton a day. It took some doing to get my butt habit down to three packs a week, the limit the law allowed.

The rule was that if you didn't have the money to buy them in the joint they'd give you three packs a week of their own brand, an old Virginia weed. But no matter how much money you had, or how many cigarettes you got sent in from outside, you could still have only three packs a week legally.

Of course trading went on. I used to give up candy, soap – anything – for cigarettes. But if you were caught trading, you lost smoking privileges. It was a constant fight to keep in cigarettes. And the rules they had were so tight that every time you got out of line you lost your cigarettes. They were tough to live by.

The only other thing I wanted besides butts was a little yarn to knit with. I got on the knitting kick fairly early and it really helped me from going nuts. I had an idea I could do it, but I really didn't know how. The girl next to me, Marietta, from San Francisco, who was in for forgery, she really taught me how in her spare time. She was a real nice dame, my only real friend in the joint. She had come from a fine home, was nice and talented and sweet. She had worked as a cashier in a restaurant, and something happened she needed some loot right away – too late to get it from the bank.

So she took it out of the till and meant to put it back in the morning. But before she could, they grabbed her and busted her, never gave her a chance, but sent her up for three years on a first-offense deal.

She was the only really intelligent chick in our cottage. Most of the rest of them were poor illiterate bitches from the South somewhere, and with them I just didn't have anything in common. I couldn't have snooted anybody if I'd tried; it was just that I didn't hit it off with anyone except Marietta. I had always been that way, one for very few people, and jail couldn't change that.

After Marietta taught me, I knitted up a storm and got real fancy. I made cable knit sweaters for Bobby Tucker and his little boy. After I got to be a wheel in the kitchen, I used to take care of Marietta by saving her the best of the food, especially when she came home for lunch.

A prison is no cinch for the warden and the matrons, either. And like the inmates and everybody else, they come good and bad. Some of them are fanatics, sure: bitches who have to feel superior to somebody and can only get their kicks by booting somebody in the ass.

But there were honest dedicated people working there who really tried to help you. And they're the ones I prefer to remember. Like a wonderful Negro matron who was really sharp and pretty-looking. They wouldn't let her wear make-up and sharp-looking dresses. She was only twenty-eight or twenty-nine. Her husband had died and she had a little girl to support. She studied and went to school and passed the exams.

She almost lost her job about eight times because she was nice and gave the girls a break. She made them go by the rules, but she was always ready to stretch a point in their favor. If the girls played records loud, she'd ask them to shut it off for the night. She had thirty-five to fifty girls in one cottage from twenty years old to sixty-five, and she handled them, and had to handle them, like a bunch of kids, whether they were whores, addicts, car thieves, forgers, murderers.

I was out and gone before the joint got famous for prisoners like

Tokyo Rose and Axis Sally. When I was in the joint the big rub was that there weren't really any celebrities around except me.

The warden and the head matron were very good to me and all the girls. The head matron quit shortly before I left; she was in her fifties, had been in the racket since 1929 and was tired. She wanted to buy a farm and live there where she could see something of her man. Don't forget, a guard has to live in prison, too, even though they get paid.

At the end, the toughest part is where they offer you all the narcotics you want. This is supposed to show whether you're really cured or not. They offered me the stuff and I found I didn't want any, and that was a great kick. But with all the doctors, nurses, and equipment, they never get near your insides at what's really eating you.

All the time I was in, this artist's representative, Ed Fishman, used to call the warden long-distance from Los Angeles every day. Fishman promised to do big things for me when I got out. I found out later he was just trying to con me into working for him, but it was great for my morale while I was in to have someone wooing me, if only in a business way.

When it came near time to get out, Fishman told me he had plans for a big concert at Carnegie. And he took over all the arrangements for my coming-out party. Fishman told me there would be reporters waiting in New York, so he suggested I get off at Newark, where he and Bobby Tucker would meet me. I wanted to duck publicity if I could.

There is nothing in Alderson, West Virginia, but a jail. If you get on a train there, you can be up to your ears in mink or you could be wearing a nun's habit, and you wouldn't fool anybody. They'd know you were just fresh out of jail. I didn't care, though, how many people knew I was fresh out. As long as I knew for sure I was. I had never cared what the hell people thought, and jail hadn't changed that none.

It seemed a long ride on the train, but finally they called Newark. When I got off, faithful Bobby Tucker, the doll, was waiting there for me, and my dog Mister was with him. I knew Mister wouldn't recognize me, or damn few others. I had gained so much weight and I just plain didn't look like the girl who had left town ten months before. I was trying to be real cool so nobody would know, in case there was anybody there looking to spot me.

Man, how cheap I played that dog! He not only recognized me, but in a flash he leaped at me, kicked my hat off, and knocked me flat on my can in the middle of that little station. Then he began lapping me and loving me like crazy.

A damn woman let out a scream. Others panicked, began to holler for the police to protect them; there were screams that a mad dog attacked a woman. Pretty soon there were plenty of lights, cameras, and action. A crowd gathered around, and my quiet incognito homecoming had blown up like a bum flash bulb. I might just as well have wheeled into Penn Station and had a quiet little get-together with the Associated Press, United Press, and International News Service.

Bobby Tucker lived with his family on a nice little farm near Morristown, New Jersey. His mother had kept what was left of my clothes and things and taken care of my personal belongings all the time, besides the dog. As soon as we broke out of the mess in the Newark station Bobby couldn't wait to take me home with him. The concert was coming up and he wanted to get right to work rehearsing.

I was scared to death. I told him I hadn't opened my mouth to sing for ten months and I didn't know what would come out when I did.

He was so sweet. He knew what I was worried about. And he knew the longer I worried the worse it would get. So he wasn't giving me any chance.

They were painting the inside of the house when we got there, and they had moved the piano out on the front porch. Before we even went inside, Bobby sat down at it.

'Night and Day' is the toughest song in the world for me to sing. So I said we'd try that first and see what happened.

I'll never forget that first note, or the second. Or especially the third one, when I had to hit 'day' and hold it. I hit it and held it and it sounded better than ever. Bobby almost fell off the stool, he was so happy. And his mother came running out of the house and took me in her arms.

We did all our rehearsing for the concert right there. We never went near New York or Carnegie. Bobby and his mother made me feel like I was home and everything was cool.

19

I'll Get By

I never fainted but one time in my life – after my midnight concert at Carnegie Hall ten days after getting out of jail.

Anybody in show business can tell you the night before Easter is the worst night of the year. It doesn't matter if you're waiting tables in a corner bar or starring on Broadway, this is the one night of the year in show business when everybody's got used to expecting no business.

And that was the night of my concert. Ed Fishman had to set the date in a hurry. There was hardly any time for advertising or publicity. But they hardly got the posters up in front of the Hall before they had to slap on the 'Sold Out' sign.

They sold space on the stage for a few hundred people, sitting and standing, which ran the gate up to about thirty-five hundred before the Fire Department called a halt. Two or three thousand people were turned away from the doors.

Backstage, of course, there was excitement and tension like I'd never seen. Both Fishman and Glaser were fighting over me. I hadn't signed with either one. My contract with Glaser had run out and I hadn't renewed it. And I didn't know enough about Fishman to take a chance and go with him.

It was only a few weeks before, people had been telling me I was through in the United States, that the public would never accept me. The mob in the street sort of answered that.

Fishman had been around before the concert was a sellout, you could say that for him. And Glaser hadn't showed his face. But then, all of the courting from Fishman wasn't what it had seemed, either.

Both agents were threatening to take me to the union, trying to prove this, that, and the other.

But all these private backstage troubles went away when I saw that audience. Nobody had told me there'd be people behind me on stage. My first thought was, 'What the hell is that big choir out there for?'

I wasn't used to this. There were as many people sitting on stage behind me at Carnegie as I would have had out front for a supper show at the Apollo.

Even before I opened my mouth to sing I had an answer for the people in Europe who told me America would never accept me after I got out of jail. And I was glad I hadn't jumped to any conclusion in jail, or run out.

By the end of the first set I was so happy and elated I didn't know what I was doing.

Just before I was set to go on for the second set a big mess of gardenias arrived backstage. My old trademark – somebody had remembered and sent it for luck. I took them out of the box and fastened them smack to the side of my head without even looking twice. I hadn't noticed, but there was a huge hatpin and I stuck it deep into my head. I was so numb from excitement I didn't even feel anything until the blood began running down in my eyes and ears.

Good old Bobby Tucker, my accompanist, saw me bleeding and almost went crazy. I'm trying to wash it out and Bobby's screaming, 'Lady, you can't go on, you must be dying.' And meantime backstage the man is calling, 'Five minutes, Miss Holiday,' and thirty-five hundred people are waiting out front. Thank God I had on a black dress, so the blood didn't show too bad. I mopped it up best I could and tried to fix my face. I sang thirty-four numbers in all. By the time I was on the thirty-third I signaled Bobby to skip 'Night and Day,' and by the time I started on 'Strange Fruit,' between the sweat and blood, I was a mess.

I made it backstage somehow. But when it came time to come out for the third curtain call I said, 'Bobby, I just can't make it no further,' and I passed out like a light.

Being around New York those first few days as a jailbird sure separated the sheep from the goats as far as my friends and colleagues were concerned. I'll never forget their reactions, and nothing can change or make me forget the way they treated me.

Friends like Bobby Tucker were always trying to take me around, get me back in the swing, pretending like I'd only been away. They worried about my morale. They knew that public acceptance is a big anonymous thing, and a girl can't live on that kind of love alone. I had to have a few hugs and kisses from people I had known intimately and helped and worked with.

So the first week I was out Bobby insisted on going to see Sarah Vaughan. She was giving a concert and Bobby took me backstage. The people hanging around there were wonderful, the air was full of 'Hi, baby' and 'oo-pa-pa-da' and everybody telling me how great I looked.

We waited for Sarah to come off between sets. I was glad to see her. And I expected she'd be glad to see me. All I expected was a little hello – after all, she was working. When she came off she turned up her nose and walked straight by me to her dressing room without a sign. To get this from someone I had worried over and tried to help really hurt.

I broke down and cried. Sarah made me wish I'd never left jail or, worse, like I was still in or carried the bars around with me.

She tried to explain later by telling me her husband, George Treadwell, had told her I was hot, just out of jail.

On the other side of the book there were people like Lena Horne who made me feel like I'd never been away.

One of those days when I was still hung over from being out of jail, I was hanging out with John Simmons of the Ellington band. John knew by ear how I felt and tried to help.

Anyway, this morning John insisted on taking me down to the Strand, where Lena was playing. I was ashamed. After my experience with Miss Vaughan, I was naturally wary. I didn't want to let myself in for another swift one in the stomach. I insisted we'd sit in the back of the theater where it was dark and just take in a rehearsal.

I should have known better. Anyway, somebody told Lena, 'Lady Day's out there.'

'Lady Day?' said Lena.

And that pretty little thing took off from that stage like a beautiful little bird. She came running down the darkened aisles hollering for me. When she saw me, she rushed up, took me in her arms, hugged me, looking at me, smiling and weeping at the same time.

'Baby, darling, why, oh why didn't you come backstage to see me?'

'Honey, don't you know?' I told her. 'I'm a jailbird.'

'Don't you say that!' she exclaimed. 'You've been sick and away for a little while, that's all.'

Then she took me by the hand, back to her dressing room. After the first show she insisted on taking me out with her and bought me lunch, and we had a wonderful schmooze about the old days in Hollywood when they gave her a bad time making this picture *Stormy Weather*. Ethel Waters had been the star of it. We talked about all this and more, and I was so happy I cried. People like Lena took the sting out of other little people.

The Carnegie concert was the biggest thing that ever happened to me. But it was difficult to top. And afterwards came the terrific letdown. I finally made my mind up between the two managers who were fighting over me. I decided to stick with Joe Glaser. Fishman was sore and left for Los Angeles.

But I soon found out the name of my manager was secondary. I could have had the greatest manager in the business, with the greatest connections in town, and still my career was out of his hands. And in the hands of the law.

Before you can work in a joint where liquor is sold you have to have a permit from the police department and the Alcoholic Beverage Control Board. This is a life-and-death matter. According to the law, which must be a hangover from the days of prohibition, nobody who has a police record can hold a liquor license. This was a sop to the WCTU at the time the law was passed. It was supposed to make sure that former speakeasy owners couldn't go legit and become saloon-keepers. But that side of the law was winked at from the beginning.

When I got out of jail they threw the book at me. My application for a cabaret card was turned down flat. Without a card no one would hire me, and there was no place I could work in New York – not if they sold juice there.

I could play in theaters and sing to an audience of kids in their teens who couldn't get in any bar. I could appear on radio or TV. I could appear in concerts at Town Hall or Carnegie Hall. That was O.K. But if I opened my mouth in the crummiest bar in town, I was violating the law. It meant trouble for me and worse trouble for the guy who owned the joint. He would lose his license and his livelihood.

That's how screwy the setup is. The right to work everybody screams about doesn't mean a damn. If I had been a booster or a petty thief I'd have the parole board helping me to get a job so I could go straight and keep straight. But as a singer, the parole board couldn't do a thing for me. It was out of their hands.

When I was really on the beach, without a police card, friends of mine tried to help me. Al Wilde came up with the idea of building a revue around me and putting it on Broadway. It seemed like a crazy idea, but he sold me. And what's more important, he sold a lot of other people to the extent of investing their loot as angels for the show. Bob Sylvester, bless his heart, invested five thousand dollars. So did a lot of other people.

We opened at the Mansfield Theater on the night of April 27, 1948. *Holiday on Broadway* was a sellout, and the first performance made us think we had a smash. The regular music critics and drama critics came and treated us like we were legit.

Working in the show with me was Bobby Tucker and his group. The two-piano team of Wyatt and Taylor opened; Slam Stewart did his stuff in the first act and Cozy Cole came on to open the second act. They used black light, which turned his drums purple, his sticks glittering yellow, and nothing showed of Cozy except his white teeth.

I did a whole book of numbers, one group in the first act and one in the second, with two fancy changes of costume. I took five curtain calls after the opening. The next morning we were reviewed in the *Times* under the head: 'Holiday Takes the Evening at Show: Billie, However, Surrounded by Galaxy of Stars of Jazz World at the Mansfield.'

It was a great idea, but we closed after three weeks.

My first club booking following the Carnegie concert took me back to a big joint in Philadelphia – the town where I had been arrested. The first night I looked out in the audience and then looked at Bobby Tucker, my accompanist, like I had seen a ghost. He didn't know what was up. But there at the ringside was Mrs Helen Hironimus, the Alderson warden. She had left her job, couldn't take it any more, and was having a fine time.

This was the first time I met anybody from the federal pen. After my second meeting with an Alderson graduate I learned to duck.

When I was playing Detroit a few years later, she came to the theater one day between shows just as I was going out shopping. She wanted to schmooze and said she'd drive me around. I knew she had been a booster, but I figured she had given it up. At least I thought she wouldn't try it when I was around.

We went into a big downtown department store. I looked at bags, lingerie, stockings. No matter what I picked out, she'd say, 'Don't buy that here, sugar. I know a place down the street where they got better stuff, and besides, it's cheaper.'

I figured she had lived there seventeen years and she should know something. So we'd move on. We had been through three stores when I finally gave up and told her I was going to buy the next thing in the next store we hit and then go back to the theater.

When we got to her car she wheeled around the corner, then stopped and began to shake herself apart. Man, that bitch had boosted everything I had looked at during the whole shopping tour. And all of it was stashed in a big pair of bloomers.

'Look, baby,' I said, 'let me out of here, and remind me never to go nowhere with you no more.'

She was hurt. She wanted to give me this whole load. She thought she was doing me a big favor.

But I figured she had just been using me, and I was so square I didn't know what was going on. 'Bitch,' I hollered at her when I left, 'if I'd gone to jail I'd have killed you and they could have had me for murder.'

So that cured me of reunions with the chicks from Alderson.

20

No-Good Man

Don't even think all the DP's were in Europe. I've been one for years. In Philly, Washington, Boston, or Frisco, I was a citizen. I could come and go, live and work where I pleased without asking anybody. Not New York.

When I had exhausted every legit way of getting my police permit to work in New York, I found there was another way. And that's where Mr Levy came in. In a way, it was the cops who introduced him to me.

In 1948 John Levy ran the Ebony Club on 52nd Street. There was somebody's money behind him, but everything was run by Mr Levy. As far as everyone knew, he was the boss. Right then all I knew or cared about was that he could give me a job when no one else dared. He was a big-time operator taking an interest in a chick fresh out of jail.

Levy was positive he could get me my police card. And when he was willing to let me open at the Ebony without one, I was convinced he knew what he was talking about.

I opened scared, expecting the cops to come in any chorus and carry me off. But nothing happened. I was a huge success. And for my first New York club date since getting out of jail, a big attraction. The Ebony was packed every night. I had Bobby Tucker and his great group backing me, and Noro Morales with his big Spanish band was on the same bill.

In the meantime Mr Levy was doing other things for me. He took me to shops like Florence Lustig's and Wilma, bought me five-hundred-dollar gowns, with gloves and shoes to match. Jewelry shops he never took me to personally. He got that stuff wholesale, but he got it, gave it to me, and it was beautiful.

I used to draw a little money as I needed it, from day to day. But I never asked for any accounting. I figured the things he bought me in a week cost twice what I was supposed to be making. And if I asked for an audit I could only end up owing Levy money.

I never had had a mink coat in my life. John Levy bought me my first one. After that I never once mentioned the subject of money again. I knew he was in my corner then. The biggest surprise of all was that he never once suggested or insisted that I go to bed with him.

He was all smooth and full of attention and good manners, but strictly business. If I started getting nervous or hinky, wondering, 'What is this?', he'd tell me to take it easy, that my manager, Joe Glaser, couldn't do anything for me and he could.

I had been living at Bob Tucker's farm out near Morristown. Then I moved to a hotel. One day he took me over to a beautiful apartment, completely furnished, and told me this was mine. Naturally I was gone after this. I thought this had to be part of a build-up and the love eyes had to come later.

I wasn't wrong.

I didn't have any guy and he knew it. When it seemed an old guy of mine might be in the picture, he fixed that. My husband, Jimmy Monroe, started coming around Ebony. I loved seeing him again. I even got to the point of thinking we might try it again and make it. But John fixed that. He not only chased Jimmy away, but did it in a way that made Jimmy seem soft and foolish and something less than what I wanted in a man. When John Levy told Jimmy not to bother me, Jimmy just chased himself off. Sure John was a big man, but nobody is that big.

John fixed it so I never wanted for anything. I had a car and chauffeur to drive me around. We went to the most glamorous clubs. Then he finished off my last resistance by buying me the first home I'd had since Pennsylvania Avenue in Baltimore. It was a fabulous place in St Albans, Queens, and we furnished it together in modern stuff and antiques, with a huge round bed like I'd seen Billie Dove have in the movies.

I even began to catch myself thinking I might be happy one day again. That, as usual, was fatal.

Trouble started when Levy booked me into the Strand Theater on Broadway. This was the start of a bunch of theater bookings at thirty-five hundred a week. The Basie band was on the bill with me, and we set some kind of a record there for a run of eight weeks on Broadway.

It was a big deal but it was work; five shows a day, seven days a week. After a few weeks you can go dressing-room crazy. The only kicks I got outside of the forty minutes on stage every three hours was when an old friend used to come backstage. We'd have lunch at the Edison Hotel or have a few in that little bar near the stage door of the Strand.

The beautiful future with Mr Levy was beginning to look like a nightmare, and there was almost nobody I dared talk to. There was nobody John Levy couldn't scare away.

I was making thirty-five hundred dollars a week, but I didn't have a nickel in my pocket. John handled all the finances, and I wasn't even allowed to draw five bucks. I was tired of it. I was embarrassed to go out and not be able to pick up the bar tab or a lunch check. So one afternoon when Mr Levy walked in I told him I wanted an allowance.

'What do you need with cash?' he hollered.

He made it sound unladylike to carry money around. All I needed to do, according to him, was whisper what I needed and he'd get it for me. I had a home, he said. I had a car and chauffeur to pick me up and take me anywhere. I had charge accounts here and charge accounts there.

'I'll give you what you need,' he told me.

The rest of the Strand run became a nightmare.

It was tough enough at the beginning. Everybody was happy about the crowds that used to flock to the theater. People were standing when the place opened in the morning. People were still standing for the last show at night. Everybody thought this was great, except me. I thought people were just coming to see how high I was. 'They hope I'll fall on my face or something,' I used to say. I wasn't buying newspaper stories. I wasn't going for any greasy damn pig.

'Some may be, darling,' they would tell me. 'But lots and lots of people out there came to see you because they love you, and don't you forget it.'

A couple of nights before I closed at the Strand, Peggy Lee sent me a message backstage asking me to come to a party she was giving at Bop City.

It was one of those tie-in deals. A magazine was going to cover it for one of those spreads. Mr Levy thought I should go. But after five shows a day I was too damn tired for any big parties. If he took me anywhere, it was more work getting ready than if I was to be presented at court – Buckingham Palace, not Centre Street. I had to be perfect – nails, hair, make-up – and it used to take me a couple of hours.

Anyway, it was a couple of hours later by the time I had finished doing myself over and Mr Levy was escorting me to the car to drive us the two blocks to Bop City.

Miss Lee had about twenty-five people at a big long table: W. C. Handy, Count Basie, Billy Eckstine. Miss Lee was seated at one end. The ball had just started by the time we got there. All the guests were expected to get up and do their stuff. Billy Eckstine was first.

As the party dragged on, Peggy Lee got up from her end of the table, came down to ours with a sheet of music. She smiled, handed it to me, and said: 'Lady, I want you to have this. I wrote this one just for you.'

I looked it over. It was called 'The Lady with the Gardenias,' or 'Gardenias in My Hair,' or something like that, celebrating the gardenia kick I used to be on, when I couldn't sing unless I had flowers in my hair.

One of the other guests looked it over, too, and then made a nasty crack.

Ice started forming all over the joint. People started rattling glasses, trying to pretend they hadn't heard what they knew damn well she said. I said 'Thank you' to Miss Lee and tried to get up and out of there.

But the plain-talking guest turned to the other people at the table. 'Well, goddamit, darlings, what's everbody so angry about? I only told the damn truth.'

But it was too early in the morning for talk as straight as this.

*

After the Strand booking probably the roughest part of my life with Mr Levy was when he walked out and left me and my goddamn band stranded in the deep South without a dime. When theater dates began to slack off, Mr Levy decided to get together a whole package show, with me as the star and fronting the band. Mr Levy had invested a little of his own money in this project, so he was playing Simon Legree all the time. The whole Savannah date was a drag from the very beginning.

This was the beginning of the end with Mr Levy, I decided. It was the end of buses and touring with bands and having to be mother superior to a group of musicians on the road.

Somebody once said we never know what is enough until we know what's more than enough. They could have had me and Mr Levy in mind.

21

Where Is the Sun?

You can get in just as much trouble by being dumb and innocent as you can by breaking the law. I've learned that the hard way. If you're doing something wrong, you *know* it and you've got at least one eye peeled looking for trouble. That way, you're in some position to protect yourself. The other way, you're just a pigeon.

I remember one time during the war I met a cat in a 52nd Street club where I was working. He was a musician and a soldier. So naturally every musician is a friend of mine from front, we don't need any introductions. We had hung out together for a couple of days before and he told me he was over the hill from some camp down South somewhere and wasn't going back. I lived in a hotel then and I took him back there with me to knock some sense into his head. I told him I'd call his sergeant on the phone and see if I couldn't fix it up for him to get back without getting into trouble. I had talked to one sergeant in my life this way and it worked. This must have gone to my fat head.

When he wouldn't even tell me the number of his outfit, I locked him in and told him to stay there while I did my evening show at the club. When I got home about four in the morning I had hardly slammed the door behind me when a couple of tough-looking white characters knocked at the door. They flashed their wallets at me, told me they were going to arrest me and carry me off for hiding a GI who was AWOL. I begged with them and pleaded with them. I told them this could ruin me, as if they didn't know. When that didn't work, I tried offering them money. I had five hundred dollars stashed in the joint. I offered them every cent if they'd let me alone and let that poor little soldier head back to camp.

They were real big about it. They took every cent, scolded me a little, and then they split. I didn't catch on until I saw them walk down the hall and exit by going upstairs instead of down. When I saw them running across the rooftops with my money, I knew I'd been had. Somebody had set me up.

Then there was that great day in January of 1949 when I arrived in San Francisco for a date at Joe Tenner's Café Society Uptown. John Levy was with me. I was miserable and unhappy but I was clean. I wasn't using anything and I wasn't thinking about using anything. If I had been, I might not have been so stupid. We had only been there a few days when Mr Levy said he had to go to Los Angeles. I drove him to the train in the beautiful new Lincoln convertible he had bought me with my money. You've never seen a car like that one. It had a bar in it, the red leather seat in the back could be made into a bed. It had a telephone, too, and in those days only doctors were supposed to have telephones in their wagons.

A day later the chauffeur drove me back to the station to pick Mr Levy up. We hardly made it back to our hotel suite when we began to argue. In the middle of it the phone rang, and I answered. It was a voice I didn't recognize asking for Mr Levy. I said, 'John, it's for you.' While I was holding the phone in my hand they hung up. In a few seconds there was a knock at the door. We were in my room, 602. I wasn't thinking about what was happening at the time. But I had to think about it plenty later, and eventually tell it to a judge and jury. Mr Levy handed me something and said, 'Billie darling, throw this in the toilet.'

When Mr Levy opened the door there were three or four white men standing there. One of them followed me right into the bathroom. There was a small hassle. The man pulled me away from the toilet bowl and tried to grab what I'd had in my hand. A government expert came into court later and testified they had found opium.

That and my record were all they had on me. But both of us were under arrest, they told us then, for possession of it. They took me out to the living room of our suite, where Mr Levy was waiting with the two other men. I knew Mr Levy had a few thousand dollars on him and I knew he would go through that old act of trying to show how big he was by trying to bribe them. I also knew it wouldn't work. I had heard of city cops taking plenty of money, but I never heard of a Treasury agent on the take since long before my time.

It was Saturday. Everything was closed. They didn't take us to jail, but directly to the police desk to be booked. When we got there, Mr Levy was still trying to buy them. That man thought money could buy anything.

Stupid me, I tried to talk sense to him. 'You're in the clear,' I told him. 'The only evidence they've got is on me. I've got one strike against me. You know what they'll do to me. I can't beat it, so let me take the rap. You can get off and go back to New York and get me a lawyer.'

When the reporters came around he said if they found anything it must have been left there by a girl who had visited me the day before.

'They just don't believe Billie gave it up,' he told them. 'They keep tailing her. Anyway, Billie used it in a different way. You never go back to smoking after that.'

The photographers kept snapping pictures of me and Mr Levy, alone and together. Without those pictures a lot of people might never know that he was a Negro. Nobody ever took me for Irish on account of my name. But with him it was different.

What the police and federal men told the reporters, I don't know. But the next day the papers from coast to coast said, 'Billie Holiday Arrested on Narcotics Charges.' Way down in the fine print Mr Levy was also mentioned. The wire-service despatches said the cops said they entered our hotel room and caught me 'in the act of using a drug.'

This was a damn lie.

Then they added a nasty sentence saying I had been 'recently released from a New York [wrong again] federal institution as "cured" of drug addiction.' And they put quotation marks around the word 'cured.' That gave the wise ones all they were waiting for.

It was Joe Tenner, boss of the club, who went to bat and called Jake Ehrlich, a famous San Francisco criminal lawyer. Mr Ehrlich recently allowed his biography to be written. My trial is included in it as one of his 'picturesque criminal cases.' I thought he was picturesque myself that day when he walked in and got me and John Levy out on bail. Joe was my friend and he was good to me, and I'm grateful to him for calling Mr Ehrlich and getting him to take my case.

Mr Levy and I were released on five hundred dollars' bail apiece, and that night I went on at Café Society. It was a couple of weeks before I was indicted by a grand jury under the state law. The charge against Levy was dismissed.

They believed this stuff was mine, just like I knew they would. They split Mr Levy out of there so fast he didn't know what was happening, just like I told him they would. The clincher was I had a record. But what I didn't know then and do know now was that he had a record too. If they'd known about that they might never have let him off. Or they might have. In view of what went down later, who can say?

After Levy left, I moved out of the hotel and went to stay with a doctor and his wife in San Francisco, who were friends of mine. They were wonderful to me and trying to help. One day he took me to a friend of his, a real estate lawyer. He never handled criminal stuff, but he was a dear friend of these friends of mine, and we got to talking about the trial.

Then someone had a bright idea. Why not have me check into a sanatorium, let them watch me, examine me, give me the tests? In twelve hours they can tell whether I'm lying or not. If I'm clean, I'll be all right. If I'm not, I'll get sick as a dog, start throwing up at both ends, and this would prove I'm a damn liar. It would be better than all the affidavits in the world. I could swear on a stack of Bibles, but who would believe me? If a doctor or a psychiatrist came in and said they watched me for a few days and never saw me sick, this would *prove* I was clean.

So I did it. It cost me almost a thousand dollars to pay the doctors to watch me and supervise me down to the last minute so they could go to court and make a statement. I stayed there four days; and when I left, everyone in the place was ready to swear on a stack of Bibles that I was clean.

That's what is so unfair about the police handling of stuff like this. If you are on and they arrest you, search you, and find nothing, they can always throw you in jail on some trumped-up charge. After they hold you there twelve hours, you'll plead guilty or sign anything to get a shot.

But this is a one-way street. If someone plants something on you and you're innocent, you have no way in the world to prove it. You can beg them to throw you in solitary confinement and throw away the key so you can prove it by not being sick, that you're clean. But they don't care. The law is the law. Technically, using drugs is not against the law; only *having* them is. This is a setup which encourages frame-ups, informers, and all sorts of dirty work.

After the indictment came down, Mr Ehrlich called me to his office for a meeting. He had seen the record of the testimony against me before the grand jury. The man in charge of the raid was the famous Colonel George H. White, an ex-OSS man, supposedly the 'ace' investigator of the Narcotics Squad. I had heard of him.

Ehrlich asked me if I had ever seen him before.

'Sure,' I told him.

'Where?' he asked.

'At Café Society Uptown, sitting at a table with John Levy.'

Ehrlich flipped. I don't think he believed me at first. I told him I could prove it. John was the type of man who couldn't resist having his picture taken with any big shot who came around. I was sure the chick who took pictures at the club must have one of him and Colonel White together. Erhlich checked. And there it was. Colonel White and Mr Levy sitting there having a drink together, big as life. Obviously the colonel wouldn't waste his time with Levy unless he was getting information.

I guess Mr Ehrlich figured this would bring me to my senses about John Levy, and it did. Unless Colonel White was wrong, John Levy was an informer on other people and bragged about it. What was there to stop him from informing on me? He had threatened often enough to turn me in. We had been fighting about money and other things.

And he had split back to New York, and I hadn't heard from him again. So this convinced me Ehrlich was right, that I had to go to the trial, go on the stand and talk.

I had to live for months with a hammer over my head, waiting for it to fall. We didn't go to trial until May 31.

Mr Ehrlich sweated over the picking of that jury. So did I. He asked each one of them if they had anything against Negroes. One woman was dismissed because she did. We ended up with six women and six men, and I was only scared of one guy. I was sure he was going to vote to hang me.

I wouldn't have known the first team from the scrubs, but Ehrlich told me the prosecutor and the judge were the best they had, and he should know.

The first witness was Colonel White. He told his story well and in great detail.

Then it was my turn to go on the stand.

How many times have I been in court in my life? It started when I was ten; then again when I was fourteen; then there are a couple times in between. One time when I was working on 52nd Street, a dressmaker brought a cheap dress in, tried to overcharge me, we got into an argument. She called me a name and I got so mad I stuck her head in a toilet bowl and flushed it. She took me to court, said I tried to drown her. But the judge listened, looked at me, and asked if she expected anyone to believe a famous lady singing star like me would do a thing like that, and that was that.

Then one time on 52nd Street after the war a cracker Navy officer at the bar had called me that same old thing. I picked up a bottle of beer, smashed it over the bar, and invited him in the street to a duel. There was a mess about that. But I came out on top.

Then there was the trial in Philly which wasn't a trial at all. And now here I was back on the stand again, telling my life story again, and scared to death again.

There were those doctors from that San Francisco sanatorium. The D.A. tried to say their testimony was irrelevant, that it didn't matter whether I used anything or not, the only thing that mattered was whether they had found it on me. But I think it impressed the jury that I had gone to this trouble to prove that I was clean. But

I knew they wanted to hear it from me. So I just busted out and told them.

'I'd been in trouble before. Two years ago. I volunteered for the narcotics cure. It wasn't for opium. But I ain't had no drugs since. I came home and society took me back. Thank God for allowing me my second chance.'

It was soon all over but the important part. The jury went out and we had to sweat it out for an hour or so, smoking in the hall-way, talking to reporters, getting my picture taken.

When the jury came in and the foreman reported 'Not guilty,' you'd think I had just finished a concert. People applauded and cheered and crowded round me like it was my dressing room after an opening.

That one cat on the jury who had worried me, the one I thought was going to vote to hang me, even he came over. He looked me square in the eye and said, 'You really didn't know, did you?'

I said no.

On the first ballot the jury had voted nine to three for acquittal. The second vote was unanimous.

And who was the first person to call me up and say, 'Darling, I'm so happy for you?'

Mr John Levy.

I didn't have carfare back, let alone the money to pay the attorney. He charged me thirty-seven hundred dollars, I think it was. John Levy had paid him a thousand or twelve hundred before he left.

John Levy offered to send me money to get back to New York. I refused. A couple years later I found out John Levy had still not paid Mr Ehrlich. Ehrlich told me he was sorry for me and I was a fool, but he wanted his money.

By then Levy was far from the scene, and this was just one of a hundred people I owed, and I arranged to pay him five hundred dollars a week.

Good old Joe Tenner gave me money enough to get back to New York. He was good to me and he had been my friend. I came back to New York the way I had so many times before, poor as the day I was born.

Those hush-hush, lowdown, confidential-type magazines can work over the story of my San Francisco trial as long as anybody cares. A while back one of them trotted out some old pictures of me in jail in Philadelphia, Jake Ehrlich in court in San Francisco, and Colonel White investigating crime with a Senate committee somewhere else. There was a big story inside. I read it. So did most of my neighbors. Then they asked me for the real lowdown inside story. I wish I knew it myself.

22

I Must Have That Man

A man can leave home one morning and come home that night whistling and singing to find there ain't nobody there but him. I left two men like that.

But John Levy had that hammer at my head. I was tied up a thousand ways. Leaving him had to be the kind of production that would make Liza crossing the ice look easy. He could always turn me in, get me busted, or hit me or something. There were bookings he had made, contracts he had signed for weeks or months in advance. Even if I could have split out I'd have been in a snowstorm of lawsuits and union charges that might have washed up my career. So I had to try to keep my head and untangle myself piece by piece, whittle down the backlog of bookings, keep him happy enough so he didn't kill me.

I was on my own. Nobody could help me.

Weeks later, while fulfilling a booking in the Brown Derby, Washington, D.C., my luck was running bad in one way, good in another. The management of the joint went bankrupt, during my run; when it came time to pay off, they couldn't make both the band and me.

This was a drag. I needed that two thousand dollars as bad as I needed any week's salary I ever made. It was my freedom money. But I couldn't take it and leave the cats of the band all hung. So I told the management to pay the band. They gave me a check that's still bouncing to this day. All the district attorneys have never been able to collect on it.

Mr Levy had said he had business in New York, so he had left. But I couldn't be sure he wouldn't turn up in the lobby of the Charles Hotel in Washington any minute.

It was cold and there was snow up to your panties over the capital. I had two thousand dollars in the hotel safe downstairs, but I didn't dare touch it. If I did I was sure someone would notify Mr Levy. He had it locked up where I couldn't touch it. He had taken one other precaution to keep me a prisoner. He had taken my mink coat and hidden it under the mattress. He was sure I wouldn't leave without that.

But I found it, put it on, put my last few dollars in a bag, put my dog under my arm, and walked out in my stocking feet down the fire escape of the Charles Hotel. I didn't have a thing except what I had on my back and that bouncing check. I split for New York with my dog looking over my shoulder.

I thought I was through with men – for sure, forever, and for keeps.

I moved into the Hotel Henry on 44th Street. I was so sure I was going to live the rest of my life there, I wanted it fixed up to suit me. It cost me $450 just to paint the joint. Then I put up drapes, got a few Chinese lamps, and kept buying things to turn that place into something that was mine – my home.

I knew I might have an affair or two here and there maybe, but anything serious – never.

My only company was a cat I liked who sometimes used to help me in and out of my gowns before I went on stage. When he wasn't doing that, he was helping himself in and out of them. We took to calling him Miss Freddy and he was always good for a laugh. He was close enough to my size, too, so a fitter or a dressmaker could work on him and not bug me. He was crazy for a lynx cape I had. It looked better on him than it did on me, too. Although the police didn't always think so. They're so narrowminded they were always picking on him for being overdressed. I'd have to go down to the station and bail him out – and whatever part of my wardrobe he had on him.

One time I loaned him my mink coat when he was going to that big annual Halloween Ball. Mrs Sugar Ray Robinson loaned her coat to a girl friend of his for the same ball. After the ball was over and they were supposed to be off the street, these two Cinderellas were hanging out in a bar someplace when the cops spotted them. They made a stand and started throwing garbage-can lids at the cops, so I had to go down again and get my mink coat out of police storage.

But Miss Freddy was good for a million laughs and never hurt anybody except himself – especially when he tried to wear my pumps.

Leonard Averhart used to come around a lot and be my handsome escort. He would stay with me for hours and keep me from being bugged.

Joe Glaser had installed Billy Sharp, the well-known band manager, as my personal and road manager. We played a few tours together, my first date in Miami at Mother Kelly's and other places. While we were playing in Canada I got sore at Sharp. We were due to fly direct to Detroit for an engagement at the Club Juana when I fired him on the spot at the airport.

I didn't have a soul I could get to take care of the endless details of these tours that drag me so. So I finally persuaded a close friend, Maely – who later married Bill Dufty – to come to Detroit with me. She went with me on Billy Sharp's ticket. She had handled other musicians, had been Charlie Parker's personal manager at one time, and she knew the ropes.

It was in Detroit at the Club Juana that I met Louis McKay again. I hadn't seen him since I was sixteen and he wasn't much older and I was singing at the Hotcha in Harlem. But during that date at the Juana, one night Louis was late getting there and I cried like a baby. So I knew my resolutions with men were going down the drain.

It got to be that way, every time I'd give up on him and cry, he'd arrive. So I finally quit fighting it, got a divorce, and we got married.

Sarah Vaughan was unlucky enough to be in an afterhours joint in Detroit that week I was there when the police raided it. With anybody else, this doesn't matter too much. So the joint is behind in its payments for protection, it can happen to anybody.

But all the cops have to do is find a celebrity, and it's page-one stuff. When I heard about it, I happened to see Jimmy Fletcher, a US Treasury agent. I went on my knees to the man.

'You're so big,' I said, 'you know everybody, do something for that girl. She's clean, she's never been in jail before. Neither have you, and you don't know what it's like. Tonight is Friday, and unless you do something she'll have to stay all weekend in the place waiting for the judge to come to work Monday morning.'

Finally Jimmy went downtown and he got her out at nine in the morning. I had Maely call George Treadwell, Sarah's husband and manager, to find out if she'd gotten out. All I wanted to know was if Sarah was all right. George said, 'Tell Billie not to worry about Sarah.'

It's the easiest thing in the world to say, 'Every broad for herself.' Saying it and acting that way is one thing that's kept some of us behind the eight ball where we've been living for a hundred years.

Louis and I came back to New York together, and we've been together ever since. I'm not going to try and say we walked off into a storybook sunset. We lived in a hotel for a while. Then we settled down at our own little place in Flushing, where we have our fights just like everybody else.

If it had been left to the managers and promoters, I could have shot myself long ago. But I've always been fortunate as far as the public is concerned. I could kill myself if it wasn't for them.

I'm still working in clubs and concerts – although if you live in New York you'd never know it. Because as I write I still have no New York police card, and this keeps me from singing in clubs in New York. People don't understand this usually; they can't believe it; but when they do, they get up and holler. So many good people have hollered about this for so long that one day the police and the Liquor Board authorities are going to have to listen. Maybe this year will be the year I'll get my card. I sure hope so.

During my years of exile from New York clubs, when I played practically no place except the Apollo or Carnegie Hall, I've been very lucky. I've played towns like Philadelphia and Chicago up to six times a year, twice a year in two or three different clubs. This is supposed to be unheard of in show business. And it isn't because managers or club owners love me. They wouldn't put up that loot unless they could fill their clubs with my friends. And I've always been grateful for that.

My friends are telling me, 'You should be rich, Lady. I just paid ten bucks for a couple of your LPs.'

I always say I'm grateful they like my songs – even those of twenty years ago. But I have to tell them it ain't going to bring me a quarter. I made over two hundred sides between 1933 and 1944, but I don't get a cent of royalties on any of them. They paid me twenty-five, fifty, or a top of seventy-five bucks a side, and I was glad to get it. But the only royalties I get are on my records made after I signed with Decca.

I've been told that nobody sings the word 'hunger' like I do. Or the word 'love.'

Maybe I remember what those words are all about. Maybe I'm proud enough to *want* to remember Baltimore and Welfare Island, the Catholic institution and the Jefferson Market Court, the sheriff in front of our place in Harlem and the towns from coast to coast where I got my lumps and my scars, Philly and Alderson, Hollywood and San Francisco – every damn bit of it.

All the Cadillacs and minks in the world – and I've had a few – can't make it up or make me forget it. All I've learned in all those places from all those people is wrapped up in those two words. You've got to have something to eat and a little love in your life before you can hold still for any damn body's sermon on how to behave.

Everything I am and everything I want out of life goes smack back to that.

Look at my big dream! It's always been to have a big place of my own out in the country someplace where I could take care of stray dogs and orphan kids, kids that didn't ask to be born; kids that didn't ask to be black, blue, or green or something in between.

I'd only want to be sure of one thing – that nobody in the world wanted these kids. Then I would take them. They'd have to be illegit, no mama, no papa.

I'd have room for twenty-five or thirty, with three or four big buxom loving women just like my mom to take care of them, feed them, see to it the little bastards go to school; knock them in the head when they're wrong, but love them whether they're good or bad.

We'd have a crazy big kitchen with a chartreuse stove and a refrigerator to match, and I'd supervise the cooking and baking. We might have a doctor and a nurse and a couple of tutors. But I'd always be around to teach them my kind of teaching – not the kind that tells them how to spell Mississippi, but how to be glad to be who you are and what you are.

When they grow up enough to go out and do baby-sitting and take little jobs or start on their own, away they'd go. And then there would always be more.

Grownups can make it some kind of way. They might have a little more or a little less to eat than the next guy – a little more or a little less love, and it isn't fatal.

But kids? Take me, I didn't ask Clarence Holiday and Sadie Fagan to get together in that Baltimore hallway and have me and then have to leave me to get pushed around and hassle with life on my own. Sure, my old lady took care of me the best she could and she was the greatest. But she was only a kid herself. Her hassle was worse than mine. She was just a young kid trying to raise a young kid.

Anyway, that's my dream and there is another dream too.

All my life I've wanted my own club. A small place where I can walk in, have my own piano, drums, and a swinging guitar. I'd want it to be crowded if there were one hundred and twenty-five people there – that's how intimate I want it.

I've fought all my life to be able to sing what I wanted the way I wanted to sing it. Before I die I want a place of my own where nobody can tell me *when* to go on. I might go on at nine, or four in the morning; I might sing forty-nine songs or one song. I might even get up and stop the band in the middle of a number and sing something I felt like singing.

But it would be a place where my friends could come and really relax and enjoy themselves – sleep if they wanted to sleep, and eat if they wanted to eat.

And I'd run that kitchen myself. I might not actually cook

everything, but I'd oversee it and taste it and see that it's my kind of cooking and that it's straight. I used to laugh when Mom talked about having her own place, but look at me now.

I could have had a dozen clubs in my time, but I'd always have been fronting for something else. Even today there are promoters willing to get behind a club of mine. But I wouldn't take somebody else's money even if they were fool enough to give it to me. I'd always be scared someone would come in and plant some stuff in my place, have me raided and busted.

Besides, it would have to be proven to me that it was mine, all mine, before the law would let me sing in it. And I would have to know it was mine before I could sing in it anyway.

Although people sometimes act like they think so, a singer is not like a saxophone. If you don't sound right, you can't go out and get some new reeds, split them just right. A singer is only a voice, and a voice is completely dependent on the body God gave you. When you walk out there and open your mouth, you never know what's going to happen.

I'm not supposed to get a toothache, I'm not supposed to get nervous; I can't throw up or get sick to my stomach; I'm not supposed to get the flu or have a sore throat. I'm supposed to go out there and look pretty and sing good and smile and I'd just better.

Why? Because I'm Billie Holiday and I've been in trouble.

Louis and I have made plenty of miles together, by train, plane, every kind of way. But I'll never forget one night when we were coming in by plane from the Coast.

When we took our seats in this big fancy air liner I knew the man next to me was going to cause a scene. I could just smell him. He started fidgeting and peeking and staring at me and Louis. He made it perfectly clear he wished he'd taken the train where he wouldn't have had to sit next to no damn Negroes.

I didn't pay any attention. This has happened to me too many times. But it bothered Louis.

We hadn't been out thirty minutes, when one of the engines caught fire. Before long the whole wing was blazing and everybody thought we'd had it.

You should have seen this dicty neighbor of ours. He got religion in a hurry. He wanted to hold Louis' hand. He wanted to be nice. He even wanted to say he hadn't meant to be nasty, he was sorry and couldn't we all pray together?

Louis had been a preacher when he was fifteen and he was ready to go along. I flipped.

'This man didn't even want to sit next to me until he thought he was going to die,' I told Louis.

'You die in your seat, mister,' I told him, 'and we'll die in ours.'

We rode out the fire someway and made the airport.

When we got on the ground, the man was so ashamed of himself he cut right on by Louis without even speaking.

'Mr McKay,' I told him, 'you've had your lesson today. Some people is and some people ain't, and this man ain't.'

That's the way I've found it, and that's still the way it is.

23

Dream of Life

I guess every Negro performer dreams of going to Europe. Some of them have gone over and never come back. Ever since I got to be a name I had thought about it too. People like Coleman Hawkins, Marie Bryant, Adelaide Hall, June Richmond and the Peters sisters had gone over and loved it so much.

Especially after six years of exile from New York clubs, with no police cards, it got to be a big thing. I used to bother Joe Glaser about it and John Hammond, Leonard Feather, everybody.

So in 1954 when the deal was actually set, and then when Fanny Holiday, my stepmother, signed those papers and I was finally able to prove I'd been born in Baltimore so I could get my passport, I still didn't believe it.

The troupe included Beryl Booker and her trio, Red Norvo and his group, and Buddy De Franco. Leonard Feather was our M.C. and shepherd.

We took off from Idlewild January 10. It was so cold the next morning when we arrived in Copenhagen, I don't believe I would have got out of bed to go meet my sister. I'd never seen so much snow or such a greeting in my life. Hundreds of people with flowers, smiling, beaming, so cheerful and happy, reporters, photographers.

We were scheduled to do about forty concerts in thirty days – sometimes two a night in Sweden, Norway, Denmark, Germany, Holland, Switzerland, Italy, and France. Then I was set to do Britain as a solo.

With a schedule like this, you know we didn't actually see much of Europe, except from a few thousand feet in the air or out the windows of a bus between planes.

But in between I met so many wonderful people who had been my friends for years, who loved me and treated me like I had come home, that I could hardly believe it.

In Copenhagen, for instance, at the airport I was introduced to a doctor who was there with his twelve-year-old daughter. They spoke English, not too good, but I could understand them. They told me how they loved me, had heard every record I ever made.

I don't make friends easily. I was polite to them, and that's about all. When the doctor heard me blowing my nose, he was all concerned. Nothing would do but I should go home with them so he could give me something for my cold. He kept at me until I finally agreed. So off we went with these perfect strangers to be guests in their home. If something like this happened at La Guardia people would say I was crazy.

You could see from their home that they had once been well off, but they had lost just about everything in the war. But they were still together, still a family. And they loved one another, you could see that. Not rich any more, just plain good people.

He gave me some medicine to soak sugar in and then swallow. It reminded me of my grandmother, who used to soak sugar in coal oil or kerosene. This stuff smelled almost the same way. I took it, and it cut all my hoarseness. And then they brought out all this crazy Danish food. Between the medicine and the food, I sang like mad at the concert that night.

It was tough to leave them. They had read about me all through the years and they loved me. And they were so sweet. They said I could come to Copenhagen and live with them any time. Keep your passport, they said, and any time you can make it, just write us and we'll send you the fare. That kind of thing would never happen to me in this country. If anybody ever met me at La Guardia Airport, I'd expect them to say, 'Send that bitch back where you got her.'

My old man Louis was the sharpest one at figuring out European money. But the thing that he couldn't figure out was an American chick who was set up over there. She was about the second soul we saw and she sold Louis a bill of goods.

She told him we couldn't speak the language, she could, and oo-pa-pa-da, we needed someone to help us, steer us around, do my shopping, be my secretary and whatnot. She wasn't going to be a maid or nothing, just help us out with all this stuff. So Louis went for it and agreed to pay her seventy-five dollars a week in addition to paying her room and board while she stayed with us in a hotel suite.

We woke up the next morning to find she'd been up since seven o'clock, ordered herself six yankee dollars' worth of breakfast, and sent her clothes out to be cleaned.

He would send her out to shop for me, to get heavy shoes or something. Everything she bought for me, she liked and bought a copy for herself, maybe in a little different color.

Louis wouldn't have a clean undershirt to his name, but she would have had all her duds dry-cleaned. One time she did try and wash out something for him. I had to wash it over again after her. The final finish came after we went out together someplace and some cat came up to her and called her Billie Holiday. She got all white in the face and flustered and explained to him that she wasn't.

But she had told us we were squares, and in a way she was right. When we let her go we had to pay her fare back to Copenhagen. I'll have to hand it to her, I bow down to her real low. She was amazing. She carried on and fooled us into thinking she was speaking these languages well, and if she can even speak decent American I'll wash out her drawers. You got to admire a smart baby with getup and go like that.

We crossed at least one border every other day, and the money was always changing. Louis bought him a book first thing. And he was the only one in the group who didn't get short-changed. He always knew what he had and what it was worth. Between Brussels and Cologne we didn't go with the group but had to make the last lap alone in a taxi that was the coldest thing I ever got into in my life.

I had a fur coat on that usually feels as if it weighs about six pounds; it didn't weigh half a pound that night, it was so cold. When the cabdriver finally got us to the concert hall all I wanted to do was get out. But the driver kept gabbing at us in German. Finally Louis said, 'What's the matter, man?'

'Goddamn Americans,' he answered.

'I gave you ten per cent, that's seventy-five cents in American money, what do you want?'

'Goddamn crazy Americans,' he said, repeating it five times.

I nearly died laughing.

Then there was Berlin. When we got there a young cat was on deck to meet us and wanted to drive us to our hotel. He took us the long way, and all the way he's giving us a sales talk.

'I have the only swing band in Berlin,' he says, just like that, in between showing us ruined churches, bombed-out homes, and the new modern buildings built over the ruins.

He kept inviting us to come to his club.

'We swing just like Charlie Parker,' he insisted.

I put him down for a real square, but he didn't give up. He kept right on our tail. Every time I took a bath I'd look around and he'd be there saying, 'Only swing band in Berlin – like Charlie Parker.' The second night we were there I couldn't stand it any more. I had to go.

I was never so happy in my life. They were the swingingest cats I ever heard. All they have is American records. The latest American sides they had were from '49 to '50, but those cats can blow. And they had to work to get that way. They're lucky enough to have no American radio or TV where some promoter can push a button and within a week every damn body is brainwashed and listening to the same stuff like 'Doggie in the Window.'

American Negro musicians have to take their hats off to them. Charlie Parker and people like him, and people like me, we just had it in us. It's got to come out someway. These cats didn't have it in them. They had to work and study and listen and work some more and get it the hard way.

And you got to give their parents credit too. They've got respect for music over there. It's culture to them, and art, and it doesn't matter whether it's Beethoven or Charlie Parker, they got respect.

If a kid of theirs comes into the world and says he wants to play, they don't act like he was a freak because he wants to be a jazz musician. They stick a horn in his mouth and they see that he gets some lessons. And those parents might be hungry, but the kids will still take lessons.

In this country, look what goes on. John Hammond came from a family rich enough to give him anything he wanted. But he was interested in jazz, so his folks thought he was nuts for hanging around Negroes. When he went around looking for talented musicians, trying to help them, he got by in the North. But in the South he had to take a sun lamp with him and try to get himself tanned enough so he wouldn't get hell beat out of him or start a riot by wandering into the Negro ghettos.

We're supposed to have made so much progress, but most of the people who have any respect for jazz in this country are those who can make a buck out of it.

I'll always remember that night in Berlin listening to those kids in their little club. I stayed until six o'clock in the morning, and the bus left at eight.

Another night in Cologne turned into a comedy when Louis didn't feel like going out and I went with Beryl Booker and her group and Buddy De Franco to jam. We were going to show them how to have a jam session. And by the time we were through, most everybody was happy, especially me.

I came home in a cab, and when I got to the hotel I realized I didn't have any money. So I told the driver to go ask the man at the desk to call my husband and tell him to pay the cab.

The cabdriver answered me back in German. I didn't understand a word, but I knew he was telling me he was going to put me in jail.

I had left the group and come on alone so Louis wouldn't be upset. And here I was stupefied, with this big cab bill. So I went to the desk myself, with the driver hollering behind me.

Then the man at the desk told me real nice that the driver was threatening to call the police and put me in jail. So I asked him real nice in English to call my husband.

He said he had, and my husband said he wasn't paying the bill. So I hollered at the driver. He hollered at me. And the desk clerk hollered at both of us.

Finally the clerk called my husband, pleaded with him to come down and break this up. He had the phone to his head when his face lit up. He turned to me and said in perfect English, 'If Madam will excuse me, Madam's husband asks me to remind Madam that Madam has money' – and he cleared his throat – 'in her bosom.'

I did. I looked, pulled it out, paid everybody off, and we were all happy.

Things were just great. I went upstairs. The door of the room was open. So I pulled myself together, stuck my hand out, thinking Louis was standing there to shake with me, and I lunged into the room.

But he wasn't. He was in the bed, not even moving.

So I kept right on lunging; nothing could stop me, I was so stupefied. I fell, and the corner of this antique bedstead hit me right in the eye.

There weren't any dark glasses in Berlin big enough to hide that eye.

The next morning, hung over as I was, with my stomach hurting, I had to climb on that bus and let everybody in the group heckle me. Nothing I could say would convince them Louis hadn't whipped me good.

But I wasn't worrying so much about them as how I'd look on stage. I tried everywhere to get make-up to cover it. There was no Max Factor in Berlin, nothing. Finally I said they must have heard of grease paint over there. And they had. I got some stuff that must have been meant for clowns in a circus. A little bit of black crept through, but I got by.

Then there was Belgium. We had a ball there, too. I went out in Antwerp with the group. Everybody was so wonderful to us, you couldn't be polite without coming home drunk. Louis was upset when I came home that way again. It was six o'clock in the morning or later. Anyway, the hotel maids were cruising down the corridors with armfuls of towels and sheets when I wandered by.

When I walked into the room I threw a shoe at him sleeping in the bed. He bounded out of bed and I ran down the hall with him hollering after me, big as he is, and not a stitch of clothes on him.

All the maids were holding their breath and chattering. So I figured I had to do something. I couldn't speak a word of whatever language they talked. But I just held my finger aside of my head, making that universal signal as if to say he was crazy.

They all smile, and they're on my side. It didn't take long for that story to spread all over the hotel – if not further. They must have told all the bellhops and elevator men and everyone that he was crazy and had fits, because no matter where Louis went the rest of the day in the hotel, somebody was ducking and dodging him like he was Typhoid Eddie.

In Berlin I met cats from behind the Iron Curtain who came across to hear our concert. One day, without knowing what I was doing, I returned the compliment.

I was wandering around the Western Zone, just rubbernecking with Leonard Feather, when he discovered we were in the Eastern Zone. He tried to talk sense to me and get me to hustle myself back into the Western sector. But hell, I figured I was already there, I might as well look around.

Leonard tried to tell me I might get into trouble. I told him I could get into trouble anywhere, there was no argument.

'I'm from Baltimore, I don't know from nothing. I want to take a look behind the Iron Curtain and see whether it's red or blue or green.' So I did, and nobody bothered us.

Then there was Zurich, where we stayed in this beautiful hotel with nothing but snow around it and white swans big as ponies floating around in a lake in front of our windows. I had never seen a pair of skis in my life, but one day Louis came in with a whole damn outfit he had bought for me, boots, pants, sweaters, and a cute little hat.

'What are you buying me this for?' I asked him. 'It's never going to get this cold in New York.'

I found out when we got into a car and drove as far as we could into the mountains. Then Louis got me out to walk and told me he had made an appointment for me to go skiing. There was a newspaperman there and a photographer and chauffeur. I didn't know it, but there was also a photographer from the American pocket picture magazine *Jet*.

I didn't know from nothing, but when I got the skis on I started liking it. After a while I got so giddy I decided to try making it downhill. I took off down the hill, fell on my can, and that, of course, is the picture everybody saw in *Jet* magazine.

We did only one concert in Paris, in a big auditorium called the Salle Pleyel. Maybe I didn't know the right places, or maybe, as they told me, I should have come back sometime in the spring. I had saved a lot of loot to go clothes shopping in Paris. But I didn't find anything I wanted to buy except underwear.

Our troupe had trouble keeping the money straight from the first day to the last. You'd have all this loot in your pocket, but it was never any good in the country you were in; by the time you'd get it changed, you were in another country. Louis kept it straight. But I didn't bother.

I just kept a pile of money of all kinds. I'd pull it out and hold this coin and bill collection in my hand and let the waiters and bartenders and other people just pick out what I owed them. Red Norvo was one of the ones who thought he knew, and look what happened to him in Copenhagen. Red came down to the hotel dining room rushing to make the bus; he had bacon and eggs, a piece of fruit, some toast and coffee, and paid the man.

When he got to the bus, our bass player pulled out one of those ruler-like gadgets they call a money calculator. He was playing with it, figuring out what this was worth and what that cost.

Red said, 'Man, what is that thing?'

He told him, and Red took it and started figuring. He adjusted it, then he flipped. 'Let's go back and get my kroners,' he hollered. 'I just paid fifteen dollars in American money for eggs and bacon.'

Red never did get it straight. He got took and took, so he had to borrow loot to make it back to New York from Paris. A real fine cat, Red Norvo.

We said good-bye to the rest of the troupe in Paris and went on to London, where I had a bunch of bookings.

For shopping, for balling, for working or anything else, give me London. To me, it's the greatest. Max Jones, the writer and jazz critic, met us there. I had never laid eyes on the man before in my life, but he knew things about me that I'd forgotten and after a few minutes I felt like I'd known him all my life. This stuff about the English reserve just doesn't go for musicians. Musicians who don't even speak the same language get to know each other real quick.

About the first thing on the London schedule was a press party Max had arranged. The newspaper people all across Europe had been wonderful to me. In the beginning I was hardly more than polite. I was so used to newspaper people in America, and the differences were amazing.

These European writers dig more music. They were hip; they had ears. The big brains, the writers and jazz authorities in America catch up with what's going on in jazz ten years after it happens. You're nobody over here until you're dead, and then you're the greatest.

Over there they write about it when it happens; they don't care how big a press agent you got, what the latest poll said, who's doing what on which hit parade; they play the records, they use their ears, and they write what they feel.

The stuff they wrote about me in Europe made me feel alive. Over here some damn body is always trying to embalm me. I'm always making a comeback, but nobody ever tells me where I've been.

Anybody who knows anything about singing says I'm for sure singing better than I ever have in my life. If you don't think so, just listen to some of my old sides like 'Lover Come Back' or 'Yesterdays,' and then listen to the same tunes as I have recorded them again in recent years. Listen and trust your own ears. For God's sake don't listen to the tired old columnists who are still writing about the good old days twenty years ago.

After a press conference in London I went out in the morning to pick up the shoes I'd left in the hall to be polished, and there was my picture on the front page, and what I told them they printed. They even got it straight and it made sense.

In London they were tops. But, as usual, it only takes one guy to put people on edge. In London it was a photographer who couldn't wait to ask me about dope. No matter what the other cats were asking me about, this one would try to get us all back on dope.

Max stepped in and said, 'Listen, man, Miss Holiday didn't come all the way to Britain to give lectures on narcotics. We're interested in music here, not dope. Even if she's on it, Britain is a civilized country where she can get to a private physician and get it legit.'

This was something I hadn't known. You just take for granted sometimes that if things are mixed up and crazy in America they got to be that way everywhere. But not in Britain, or most of Europe either. Sick people who are on stuff over there are treated like sick people. They go to their own doctor and he gives them what they need. If he can help them get off, he does, by gradually lowering the dose. If he can't he keeps them in shape by giving them what they need to go on working and living a normal life. Nobody has to risk his life by going to the black market and paying a hundred bucks for something worth four cents – and then getting stuff that's so bad it's liable to kill you. There's little if any black-marketing or profiteering. People don't have to go out shoplifting, mugging, or robbing one another to get money to buy stuff this way!

Americans used to make fun of the British health system, where sick people could go to doctors and hospitals for free and the government picked up the tab. We laughed about them handing out false teeth and wooden legs for free. We hollered about this being government interference with the practice of medicine.

Well, let me tell you, in America if they haven't got government interference in medicine I don't know what it is. If you're on and you get a doctor for help, he can't help you because the government has passed out regulations saying, in effect, that if he does he will go to jail along with you. If you go to the doctor, he's liable to slam the door in your face and call the cops.

Most countries in Europe are civilized about it and they have no 'narcotics problem' at all. One day America is going to smarten up and do the same thing.

It may not even happen in my lifetime. Whether it does or not is no skin off mine, because I can't possibly be hurt any more than I have been. But for the sake of other people who've got to suffer until the country wakes up, for the sake of young kids whose whole life will be ruined because they are sent to jail instead of a hospital, I pray to God that we wake up soon over here.

All you have to do is look at the story of my life. If there's any moral at all in it, it's this:

If you think dope is for kicks and for thrills, you're out of your mind. There are more kicks to be had in a good case of paralytic polio or by living in an iron lung. If you think you need stuff to play music or sing, you're crazy. It can fix you so you can't play nothing or sing nothing.

The only thing that can happen to you is sooner or later you'll get busted, and once that happens, you'll never live it down. Just look at me.

I don't want to preach to nobody. I never have and I don't want to begin now. But I do hope some kids will read this book and not miss the point of it. Maybe because I have no kids of my own – not yet – I still think you can help kids by talking straight to them.

If nobody can learn from the past, then there's no point in raking it up. I've raked up my past so I could bury it. It's worth it if just one youngster can learn one thing from it.

On a recent Sunday, Judge Jonah Goldstein talked about the narcotics problem on TV from New York. He told the people the same thing I've been trying to tell them; that narcotics has to be taken out of the hands of the police and turned over to the doctors. He said that in all his years on the bench he'd never seen anybody but poor people brought before him for violation of the dope laws.

He also said a man had come to him for advice recently because his twenty-year-old son had been hooked on dope. What did the judge advise him to do? Send the boy to England to school where doctors could treat him legally, cure him if they could, and if not, give him treatment legally just as if he had diabetes or something, so he could live a useful normal life.

That's a hell of a recommendation for a judge to have to make in a civilized country; to admit that the only help a sick person hooked on drugs can get is outside this country; to admit that the only civilized way of handling the problem is to go somewhere else – if you're lucky enough to have the loot. It's sad but it's true.

When I got hooked I was unlucky all round. In the first place, I didn't know there was any such way of getting help. I didn't know the civilized way they handled this thing in England and in most of Europe. Even if I did know, there was a war on and no damn way for me to get to England except to swim or join the WACs.

But maybe some of the kids who wouldn't be caught taking advice from a judge will listen to me. I sure hope so. Dope never helped anybody sing better, or play music better, or do anything better. Take it from Lady Day. She took enough of it to know. If anybody ever tries to tell you that, you ask them if they think they know something about dope that Lady Day don't know.

I think that my getting hooked on dope killed my own mother. It sure helped, anyway. And I think if a child of mine got hooked it would kill me. I don't have the strength to watch anybody else go through the torture I went through to get clean and stay clean.

All dope can do for you is kill you – and kill you the long slow hard way. And it can kill the people you love right along with you. And that's the truth, the whole truth, and nothing but.

The night of my big concert in London was the biggest thrill of my life and the biggest place I ever worked. A thirty-four-piece band to back me. Wow! And the audience? They don't get them like that at the Metropolitan Opera in New York. After I was introduced you could have heard a pin drop in that huge place. You could hear my heels clicking on the floor as I walked to the center of the stage.

And when I was through, there was beautiful applause like you never heard in your life.

Another thing they do over there that made sense; you do three concerts in one night. One for an audience of youngsters; the second a big one for a regular mixed audience. And then the concert pro-moter has a night club where you work afterwards. This gives you a chance to dig everybody – kids, high hats, and people that drink – all in one night.

Then we did shows in small towns just a few minutes' run on the train outside of London.

Only one thing gave me trouble in London, that was the food. I got so tired of fancy hotel food, one night I took out a little can of red beans that I'd carried all the way over there with me. I got me some garlic, some hamburger meat. I took out a can of Sterno and started cooking up a batch of red beans the way I like them. About enough for three people.

I thought I was going to get thrown out of the place for making a stink, but before the stuff was done I had the maids, the assistant managers, the elevator boys all fighting over it. We had a ball.

I should have known something like this would happen. Almost twenty years before Hugh Panassie, the big French jazz authority, came over to America, I met him at Irene and Teddy Wilson's. He flipped over my red beans and rice and I had to give him a big case of dried red beans to take back with him.

I'm still sending dried red beans to people in London.

24

God Bless the Child

'Well, Billie, you're back again. We been expecting you. You know you won't get a thing in here.'

It was the old woman doctor in the Philadelphia jail again, yapping good morning just before dawn on Thursday, February 23, 1956. She seemed unhappy because she hadn't seen me – without paying – for nine years.

I straightened her wig right off. 'I ain't asked you for nothing and I'm not likely to. But you can't even wait until I do before you tell me no.'

She was talking about dope and I knew it. But I was talking about human kindness and she knew it. Sure, I'd been busted again. And I was in jail. But nothing she could say or do could bug me. This went for the whole crew – the fuzz who busted in my hotel room, the magistrate sitting on his bench at dawn waiting for me to come on, the police inspector putting out big stories to the papers, the cameramen flashing those bulbs in the face of my little two-pound Chihuahua Pepi as he led me into the clink on his leash.

I knew the papers would say: 'What, again?' It might look like just old times, but it wasn't. There was a big difference. I didn't feel lost. I didn't feel alone. And I wasn't alone. Louis was with me. They carried us off together and Louis held my hand and whispered: 'Lady, don't you worry about a thing. You and I are going to beat this thing. And I'm going to take care of you and see we do.'

God has blessed you when he lets you believe in somebody. And I believed in Louis.

I had worked that week at the Showboat in South Philadelphia. We stayed at a little hotel around the corner in a room with a kitchenette. After the last show Wednesday night, sometime after 2 AM when they closed the joint, Louis and I walked home. I had undressed, fed Pepi, and was standing there in my drawers with a little pot of lima beans in my hand. Somebody turned the key in our door from the outside, so quiet like it had been greased. I never heard a thing until I saw four men and a woman standing there with a warrant. Louis talked to them, looked over their papers, saw they were legit. He was cool and gentle as a lamb. He asked me to get dressed and go with them. He didn't like what I started to put on. He reminded me the photographers were waiting, and asked me to put on something prettier.

The first thing they did, like they always do, is to lock the toilet bowl so it won't flush. Then they started searching the place. The bathroom was about the size of an overseas trunk, but they wouldn't even let me go in there alone. The plain-clothes woman climbed in there with me. Lucky for her she was skinny and didn't take up too much room.

Before they were through they ransacked everything we owned; they threw around my gowns, looked through my coats, my shoes, my underwear; poked in my make-up; they looked in the dog food, under the rug, behind the drapes, in the bed and under it. The plain-clothes woman searched my body, looked in my ears, under my bra and my girdle. They turned Louis' linings inside out the same way. But there was nothing there.

They found Louis' gun smack on the top of his suitcase. That's where he keeps it so it couldn't be missed. He seemed relieved about that. He had told me a hundred times that if the local law ever went out on a limb to arrest me and couldn't turn up any evidence, the gun would give them something to save face with. He thought they would arrest him for carrying the gun without a permit; he could take the rap and it would be easier than causing them the trouble of trying to get something on me that could be made to stick in court.

Don't forget, the law knows where I live and I've never once been arrested in my own home. Not even in my dressing room. It's always in some public hotel. Louis has always searched every hotel room the first minute we check in, to find if anything is stashed there. In Los Angeles once he found three reefers on the ledge at the top of our windows and threw them out. Those three reefers would have been enough to put both of us in jail. If you've been arrested before for narcotics, you learn to live that way. And Louis spent a good part of his time on the road trying to protect me.

But you never know. You can leave a hotel to do a show. Anybody can come in the room while you're away, either to look for something or to leave something behind – something they can come back and look for later. That's why Louis was so happy when they found his gun. He hoped they'd settle for busting him. But they didn't find a bit on him. All they can claim is that they found evidence in our room. We'll see about that when we have our day in court.

In this country, don't forget, a habit is no damn private hell. There's no solitary confinement outside of jail. A habit is hell for those you love. And in this country it's the worst kind of hell for those who love you.

Many a sweet time Louis has risked his own life to try to help me. Husbands, wives, mothers, and fathers of addicts do it every day. And in this country, this makes them criminals.

I can tell you about a big-name performer who had a habit and a bad one. There were times when he had it licked. And other times it licked him. It went around that way for years. He was well known, like me, which makes it worse. He had bookings to make, contracts to fulfill. In the middle of one engagement he was about to crack up and go crazy because he had run out of stuff. There was no way in God's world he could kick cold turkey and make three shows a day. There wasn't a doctor in town who would be seen looking at him. His wife got so scared he'd kill himself that she tried to help him the only way she knew – by risking her own neck and trying to get him what he needed. She went out in the street like a pigeon, begging everyone she knew for help. Finally she found someone who sold her some stuff for an arm and a leg. It was just her luck to be carrying it back to her old man when she was arrested.

She was as innocent and clean as the day she was born. But she knew that if she tried to tell that to the cops it would only make her a 'pusher' under the law, liable for a good long time in jail. She thought if she told them she was a user, and took some of the stuff in her pocket to prove it, they might believe her, feel sorry for her, go easy on her. And she could protect her man. So that's what she did. She used junk for the first time to prove to the law she wasn't a pusher. And that's the way she got hooked. She's rotting in jail right now. Yes siree bob, life is just a bowl of cherries.

I've had my troubles with the habit for fifteen years, on and off. I've been on and I've been off. As I said before, when I was really on, nobody bothered me. I got in trouble both times when I tried to get off. I've spent a small fortune on stuff. I've kicked and stayed clean; and I've had my setbacks and had to fight all over again to get straight.

But I'm not crazy. I knew when I started to work on this book that I couldn't expect to tell the truth in it unless I was straight when it came out. I didn't try to hide anything. Doubleday carried an item in their winter catalogue that I was writing about my fight with dope and that I knew it wasn't over yet. There isn't a soul on this earth who can say for sure that their fight with dope is over until they're dead. *Variety* printed an item about it a couple of months before. I've been under a doctor's care and treatment before I went to Philadelphia and since. So what did the police down there think they were proving when they used me for a pigeon? You tell me.

Anyway, they brought me and Louis to the magistrate, who was waiting for us. Both of us were booked for 'possession and use,' under their local laws – the same laws that let them arrest people for carrying benzedrine tablets across the city line. And Louis was booked for possession of that pistol without a permit. They slapped a high-assed old bail of seventy-five hundred dollars each on us. In a lot of places you can kill somebody and get sprung for less. Louis told them he'd been arrested years before in Pennsylvania when he was a delinquent kid. He'd done some time for it, too – one more thing we have in common. Both of us can split a match four ways, that's one of the important things you learn in jail. So the police pulled out his card file with the picture on it of the way he looked as a kid. Naturally they made a big thing of that and announced it to all the papers. Then we were hauled over to the Philly county jail. It's got two entrances. One is marked 'His' and one 'Hers.'

I begged the matron to let me keep my money and my clothes. I've only been to the fifth grade, but I know a few things about jails they don't teach you in school. Once they get your clothes put away and your valuables locked up, there ain't no bondsman on earth can get them out for you in a hurry.

I told them I didn't have nobody to take care of Pepi, so they let me keep him in the cell with me. He gave them a hard time. He was so little he could slip out between the bars, and they knew it. Every matron or turnkey that came by, Pepi would bark up a storm. There were some things in there, crying and screaming as they took the cold-turkey cure on the cement floor. Every scream that came from outside, Pepi would bark back.

There was nothing in the cell but a toilet and a long plank to lay down on. Pepi is so delicate he would get pneumonia in a minute, so I was busy worrying how to keep him warm. I spread my blue mink coat on the board and used it for a mattress while I cuddled that dog to keep him warm. But it wouldn't work. We were cold on top. So I pulled out my mink and threw it over us. Then we were cold on the bottom. When I wasn't worrying about Pepi, I was worrying about Louis on the other side without any topcoat. But the men in that jail treat each other better than the women do.

I had been on my feet since nine-thirty the night before when I went to work, and I was beat. But I couldn't even catch twenty winks in that place.

They only let you make one phone call. I used it to call a friend in Philly and ask her to start scrounging for the thousand dollars or more it would take in cash to get me and Louis out on bail. The ban on telephone calls wasn't too tough on me. Newspapers are good for one thing – they let your friends know you've been busted.

It was five o'clock that night before the bondsman got me out. I walked out of that jail and went back to the hotel. That little one room looked like a cyclone had hit it. I got on the telephone and arranged to get an advance on my salary so I could get Louis out.

Then I pushed a pile of my gowns off the bed, fed Pepi, and tried to take a nap.

In a few minutes two friends from New York came in the hotel. They got me something to eat and a drink. By the time I fixed my hair and found a dress that hadn't been pawed into a mess of wrinkles, it was time for my first show to go on.

The club was packed. Most of them were customers, but a lot of them looked like fuzz. I closed my first set with 'My Man.' If the customers didn't know from reading the papers that Louis was still in jail, the fuzz did. They told me I'd never sung it any better. I'm sure I never felt it more.

At least one member of the Vice Squad was caught with a tear on his cashmere coat. But they recovered after the show and took my accompanist off, shook that poor boy down, made him take his clothes off, and looked in all his wrinkles to see what they could find. When I saw them carrying off that boy, I felt so sorry for him and so helpless I was ready to cry. When they couldn't find nothing on him, they let him go. It was real big of them.

Then I went to the office and made a deal with the bondsman. He found a judge to sign the paper, then he drove over to the jail to spring Louis. When I came off after the second set, Louis was waiting in my dressing room.

When I finished that show, I couldn't wait to get out of town. I couldn't stand the sight of that hotel room one more night. I had to sleep and I couldn't sleep there.

We took a taxi to the station. Luck was still with us. There'd been a big train wreck near Washington, and there'd be no trains before morning. The station was deserted. There was hardly anybody there but the fuzz. They looked as tired of watching me as I was of them.

Louis tried to negotiate a connection on a bus.

The best we could do was a couple of single seats on a crowded bus. It took me back twenty years, to be heading back to New York the way I had so many times before: busted, out on bail, broke from paying the bondsman, hungry from having no time to eat, beat from twenty-four hours without sleep, remembering the smell of that jail as I rattled around in a damn bus with a sleeping sailor falling all over me. But all that I soon forgot, with my man.

This time, the doctors have told me, with any kind of luck, I should be able to stay straight for two whole years. Who can ask for anything more? I've got enough of that Fagan Irish in me to believe that if the curtains are washed, company never comes. If you expect nothing but trouble, maybe a few happy days will turn up. If you expect happy days, look out.

But no doctor can tell you anything your own bones don't know. And I can let the doctors in on something. I knew I'd really licked it one morning when I couldn't stand television any more. When I was high and wanted to stay that way, I could watch TV by the hour and loved it. Who can tell what detours are ahead? Another trial? Sure. Another jail? Maybe. But if you've beat the habit again and kicked TV, no jail on earth can worry you too much.

Tired? You bet. But all that I'll soon forget with my man . . .